THE
Bombshell Bible

The Only Makeover Book
for *Style* and *Soul* ...

BY
JACQUELINE **BRADLEY**

The Bombshell Bible
The Only Makeover Book for Style and Soul ...

By Jacqueline Bradley ©2005

For copies of this book or permission to reproduce, please contact the author:
Jacqueline Bradley
www.thebombshellbible.com

Published by

TBC Publishing

Printed in Canada

Library and Archives Canada Cataloguing in Publication

Jacqueline Bradley, 1971-
The Bombshell Bible:The Only Makeover Book for Style and Soul,

Jacqueline Bradley

Includes bibliographical references
ISBN 0-9737228

1. Relationships   2. Self Help   I. Title

To my mother Margaret and grandmother Rose.
And to my littlest Bombshells Berkley and Rielle.

TABLE OF CONTENTS

Acknowledgements vii

Foreword: *The Birth of a Bombshell . . . And Bombshell Coach* xi

Chapter One: *Bombshells Are Made, Not Born*..................................... 3

Chapter Two: *From Boredom to Bombshell* 15

Chapter Three: *Working Up to Working Out*.. 31

Chapter Four: *Smiling—The Super Easy Superpower* 43

Chapter Five: *Let Your Light Shine*.. 51

Chapter Six: *Carriage—Not Just Locomotion* 59

Chapter Seven: *Finding the Perfect Fit*... 67

Chapter Eight: *Restoration Work, Anyone?* 83

Chapter Nine: *Making an Entrance and Leaving an Impression* 91

Chapter Ten: *That Thing You Do—The Signature Move* 107

Chapter Eleven: *Find Him, Get Him, Keep Him . . . If He's Worthy* 119

Chapter Twelve: *Bombshells and the Company They Keep*.......... 131

Chapter Thirteen: *Because Happiness is Contagious*...................... 141

Chapter Fourteen: *Keeping the Faith and Giving it Back* 157

Chapter Fifteen: *Showing 'Em What You've Got* 165

Chapter Sixteen: *Bombshell Forever* 173

Afterword: *It's a Bombshell's World* 177

ACKNOWLEDGEMENTS

Without the inspiration of my mother Margaret, and grandmother Rose, I would not have been able to inspire others. Dear Mom, just being in your presence enriches my being endlessly. Also to my father Wayne: Dad I thank you for the gifts of laughter, love and forgiveness. To my sister Angela whose talents I admire more than she knows, many thanks for allowing me to experience your ever expanding embrace. Keep it up my little fairy for you have no idea the self- love that awaits you! To Maddy, sister two, you are one of our girls in every way and are a joy to our family. To my brothers, Kirk, Andy, Wayne, Paul, David and little Paul. The lessons learned by each of you in different ways afforded me a love and respect for all men. In such diverse ways, you are truly wonderful men who have each had hands in helping me celebrate my inner Bombshell. To Grandma Course and her strength. To Dr. John, I have felt your acceptance of me as one of your own and will not forget your generosity of spirit to us all. To Pinky, thank you for waiting and Grant: oh the love you've taught me and the love I have for you both!

To Mum and Dad Bradley and family.

To my friends Vesna, Isanne, Caleigh, Huw, Faith, Warren, Mikey (head of Bombshell logistics), The Shvartsmans (Who's the best?) and Jenn (We miss you Jenn).Each of you has walked beside me and allowed me walk beside you in a winning life team-thank you. You are women of true Bombshell status that I have been blessed to have as friends. To Martha, always bright always believing, always good and wise beyond her years! To Kylie (and Bobby) thank you for your faith and for getting my message.

To Barb, thank you for allowing me to help you uncover the spectacular Bombshell within you and thanks for being my friend; I love you dearly. To Jamie...exactly what all men should be when they grow up, filled with love and integrity. You are a gift my love.

To my nieces and nephews, Bay, Ava, Byron, Brayden, Johnny, Mitchell, Christopher, Nicholas, Matt, Nicky, Devon and Sarah. To Brittany, Hannah, Morgan, Ashley, Cheyenne and Shyla.

To Dave a.k.a Daddy, thank you for the gifts of our children and for being my best friend always. You are a very special, wonderful man and the father of any child's dreams.

To all the women seeking their inner Bombshell...keep looking, it is in all women and you will find yours. When you do uncover yours let it shine, it will be your gift to the world!

To my littlest Bombshells and the shining stars of my universe, my daughters Berkley and Rielle: you are the truest loves and the most radiant beauties, the sound of your laughter is like the tinkling of bells to my soul. I love you magically and endlessly and look forward to seeing you become the world's greatest Bombshells!

FOREWORD

The Birth of a Bombshell . . . And Bombshell Coach

People always ask me what "it" is; they want to know how and why certain women quite literally light up a room. Many misconceptions are born from this curiosity. "It must be her outfit, perhaps her perfume, or maybe it's the implants that everyone seems to be sporting these days," are the types of comments I hear. The sad but true fact is that people are frightened by the things they don't understand.

Have you seen the woman I am referring to? She enters the room and everything seems to stop. Everyone watches where she is going, who she is sitting with and even what cocktail she orders. She smiles radiantly, like everyone is expecting her, as though they have been eagerly awaiting her arrival. Owners of establishments leap to greet her and kiss her warmly on both cheeks, proudly displaying their familiarity to all who are looking on. Other women become visibly agitated and hold a little tighter to their husbands or boyfriends—not that this woman is even looking at them.

She is attractive, maybe even beautiful. She is not physically flawless, but you can't put your finger on anything that is out of place—her imperfections are lost in the haze of her positive energy. People whisper that they have seen her somewhere before: on television or in a magazine, but the reality is that she only acts famous. She feels special, sparkling within herself for people to love or hate—whatever it may be, it does not adversely affect her because she feels wonderful about herself and she emanates her confidence. It is an almost palpable sense of self that attracts people to her. She laughs generously and smiles at and kisses other people's children just for a love of the human spirit.

She owns her beauty and knows that the most powerful aspect of her beauty is that which resides within her soul. It is her gifts of confidence and self acceptance that become the unshakeable foundation of the true Bombshell. It is the white noise of the Bombshell that sounds like music to others. She is the woman that other women can look to for inspiration and guidance and a calling that she fulfills with ease and enthusiasm.

This woman is the consummate Bombshell. Achieving her position is not hard if you believe that this is a journey you wish to embark on. By learning to display this confidence that you admire so greatly, you can become the woman that you have always wanted to be. Everything you need to achieve this already exists within you. Let me show you how to make it shine.

CHAPTER ONE

Bombshells are Made, Not Born

CHAPTER ONE
Bombshells are Made, Not Born

To have sex appeal without great personal strength as a woman is to wield a weapon that will inevitably be turned against you. This is the greatest difference between a successful Bombshell like Audrey Hepburn and an unsuccessful one like Marilyn Monroe.

A successful Bombshell is made up of sex appeal and a strong spirit knowing that to venture too far from a healthy balance would be unwise. She is exceptionally confident, strong, sure of herself and can carry her sexuality with pride. The Bombshell does not allow her sex appeal to define her, but rather refuses to deny its existence. I want to help you realize that your strength comes from within, your beauty is from your soul and worthy of celebrating. The gifts that you already possess are endless; yours alone to give and when you finish your Bombshell transformation you will know how to embrace and utilize those gifts. But be careful; you can easily fall victim to those trying to undermine your power as a woman and a true Bombshell won't let that happen!

Poor Beautiful Marilyn

Certainly one of the world's most renowned Bombshells was Marilyn Monroe and there is no denying her stunning beauty and sexual allure, so what went wrong? By all accounts, the ghosts that haunted this young woman were much stronger than all of the wealth and fame in Hollywood. Born Norma Jeane Mortenson on June 1, 1926, to an emotionally unstable mother, the future Marilyn's life did not start out glamorously. Essentially abandoned as a girl, she began her quest for belonging at a very young age. Being shuffled through orphanages fueled her childhood insecurities and she was unable to find what the human heart most desires: love and acceptance. Like all young girls Norma Jeane longed to feel wanted, needed and unconditionally loved—not such a tall order if you have already come to love and accept yourself, but tough to achieve when you tread on territory that is unfamiliar to your soul.

By the time she hit her teenage years, Norma Jeane knew she was pretty, she even knew she was sexy, but she had no idea that she was worthy. She didn't understand that she deserved the genuine adoration of her fans and the people in her personal life. Married at a young age to the boy next door, Norma Jeane saw marriage as an escape from herself, not as a joining of souls. To be able to feel a sense of security she felt she needed to be married. When her husband left to fulfill his duty to his country by serving in the Merchant Marines, Norma Jeane decided it was time to stand on her own two feet, and in true Bombshell-style she got herself a job. Working on an assembly line was where Norma was discovered—the photographer could not believe he had found such a beautiful and uncultivated talent. Unfortunately, this may have been her undoing, for Norma had been discovered by someone else before she had discovered herself. You see dear Bombshell, if a woman has already given herself a healthy emotional appraisal, she will be far less likely to accept anything less than what she believes herself to be worth.

Marilyn is quoted as saying, "I knew I would belong to the public, not because I was beautiful or talented, but because I never really belonged to anything else." This speaks chilling volumes about her lack of self-esteem. You see, if you don't have an unwavering belief in yourself, then anyone can impose their opinion on you and you will never truly know who you are and what you are capable of achieving. After changing her name to Marilyn Monroe and undergoing a drastic makeover, a frightening realization began to plague this glamour-pot: she still did not know why she wasn't happy with herself. Clearly Marilyn had only uncovered her external beauty and despite her loving nature, she never found strength in who she was as a woman.

At some point in Marilyn's life she needed to clean her "emotional laundry." What I mean by this is that her difficult childhood and overnight fame and fortune left her feeling shaken and her emotional infrastructure needed to be addressed and dealt with before she moved forward in her adult life. It is clear that Marilyn's fragility can be attributed to her childhood, but undeniably, living in the past is a choice we make. Marilyn had to make decisions in her life that would allow her to become a stronger, better woman and could possibly have made her the ultimate Bombshell of our time, but instead she opted to give that control to the people around her in an attempt to find love and acceptance. If she had taken stock of her personal qualities and potential, she may have realized that she could have been sexy, smart, strong and in control of her own destiny. Knowing that she could be in complete and total control of her life was her power as a woman and it would have made her unstoppable in life and love.

Audrey Hepburn: A Bombshell Success

Fair Audrey is the perfect example to show you that a Bombshell is not always buxom and blonde! Born on May 4, 1929, to a Dutch baroness and a wealthy English banker, Audrey was destined to lead a charmed life. Or was she? Her parents divorced when she was very young and Audrey and her mother moved to The Netherlands. Not long after this, the young Bombshell labored through the Nazi occupation of Holland, leaving Audrey to suffer from severe starvation, anemia and respiratory problems. While it is clear that Audrey came from a family of some wealth, she could not buy her way out of this one; this was one challenge she would have to fight with her inner strength. So many people who have suffered traumatic oppression and illness carry this with them in life to be used as an excuse for failure, but not this Bombshell.

Following the end of the Nazi occupation, young Audrey moved to London with her mother. Though she studied dance, Audrey was discovered by a French novelist and cast as the lead in *Gigi*, despite not having previous acting experience. She acknowledges her good fortune: "I probably have the distinction of being one movie star who, by all laws of logic, should never have made it." She makes it clear that she was aware of her inexperience in the industry and in the Hollywood of large-breasted blondes she knew the odds were not in her favor. So what was it that made her successful?

Audrey had a mother of incredible strength and I am sure that this is part of the reason for her success. The mother is the greatest teacher in any child's life and Audrey was fortunate enough to have one who would do anything for her child's well-being, including working in the resistance of World War II. This was unheard of at the time and Audrey would even help out by delivering covert messages via her ballet shoes! So despite coming from a "broken home" and enduring the atrocities of the ugliest war that history has ever seen, this young girl and her mother remained filled with strength and integrity. They are a good example of progress: one good teacher showing one good student the ropes and allowing Audrey to become a true Bombshell.

You see, Audrey became a Bombshell in every sense, maintaining herself as a star and as a woman, never selling out to the pressure of Hollywood's idea of beauty. From 1953 to 1967 Audrey starred in scores of successful films and was nominated for four Academy Awards. Eventually she would marry twice and have two beautiful children while maintaining her Bombshell status, including when her career was on hold and she was taking the lead with her family. Nothing in Audrey's life was typical and clearly she was gifted in many ways, but the truest gifts she possessed were those of the intangible variety. The intestinal fortitude she displayed allowed her to blossom in all areas of her life despite a seeming lack of experience and some of life's frightening challenges.

The most profound thing about this brunette Bombshell was the control she had of her life and career. Her beauty was overshadowed only by her ability to give back to the world in every way. Audrey's immense contributions to children's causes ensure that this Bombshell will live on. Although she has now left us, we continue to celebrate her life because the only tragic thing about Audrey was the void created by her departing this world. She left the world loved, accomplished and totally fulfilled as a woman. Now that is a Bombshell.

Diana, Princess of Potential

Diana, Princess of Wales, had all the makings of a Bombshell. Born into British aristocracy and a happy, loving family, Diana had a glorious beginning. The apple of her father's eye and afforded every opportunity to achieve greatness, life for this shy, beautiful girl should have been long and charmed.

In what Diana believed was a dream come true, she married her proverbial and literal Prince Charming in 1981. A fairy tale to those on the outside looking in, Charles and Diana should have lived happily ever after. Sadly for Diana, once her life was plucked from the safety of her family and placed squarely in the lap of the monarchy and the public, she began to spiral downwards into what would ultimately be a sad and deadly demise. This was certainly not what the world wished for such a caring, kind and obviously compassionate woman but sadly was the path chosen by this wavering Bombshell.

As we all know, the Prince and Princess had two stunning boys and Diana proved herself to be a fiercely protective and loving mother, continuously juggling her duties as princess and parent while trying to save her faltering marriage. Few of us can understand the pressures of intense scrutiny Diana endured; and let's face it, the very things that made her an embarrassment to the royal family endeared her further to the general public. The British tabloids were (and still are) relentless in their pursuit of Diana and that only exacerbated her public pain and humiliation.

This is not a new story. Many before Diana have held themselves against the paparazzi and the demise of a marriage to a man like Charles. The difference between Diana and a successful Bombshell comes down to only one issue, and of course it is the most important of them all. Diana lacked the fundamental sense of self that stays with the Bombshell her entire life once it is discovered. It is this unshakeable sense of internal strength that would have turned Diana's story from tragic to triumphant. She was looking desperately for support in all the wrong places and seemed to overlook her own power as a woman that was waiting for her in endless supply.

If Diana had taken the time to cultivate her womanly gifts, she would have been able to stop running and hiding because it turns out that the only person she was running from was herself. She illustrates beautifully that to amass such qualities as kindness, compassion and a strong maternal instinct is tenuous when placed upon the precarious perch of insecurity. There are many elements to a Bombshell's success, but clearly all of the others combined cannot compensate for the lack of internal development of one's self as a confident woman. She was shining out a spotlight seeking support instead of becoming a beacon and letting her light flow in a way that was indicative of her inner beauty and would have attracted a healthy, natural life team to rally around her.

Diana's story is one that could potentially teach all women a lesson in self-awareness and strength. Had she stopped running long enough to take emotional stock of herself and remember all of her special gifts that could never be taken from her, Diana's life would have been long and legendary as opposed to the legacy of sadness left behind for her beautiful boys and the world who loved her.

Jackie O and Camelot

Probably the most notable modern-day Bombshell, the beautiful and well-raised Jacqueline Lee Bouvier learned early that her grace, intelligence and confidence would be the most important tools in her life. She knew that they were not to be taken by anyone but could be admired by all.

Born to affluent parents in Southampton, New York in 1929, Jacqueline seemed destined for a flawless life. Sent to the most exclusive private schools and given exposure to the most elite friends and activities, one could say that she was the perfect candidate to become the consummate Bombshell. Not a stunning beauty, but classic and mysterious-looking, Jacqueline always carried herself like a lady—a natural talent for her. Jacqueline's obvious intelligence led to her meeting one of the most influential men in the country, John Fitzgerald Kennedy. The true test would begin for this Bombshell following her 1963 marriage to the future President of the United States.

Jackie's life changed radically when, at age thirty-one, she became one of the youngest first ladies in American history and was thrust into a spotlight that would shine obtrusively into her life until her death. Amazingly, this intensely private Bombshell rose to the challenge with a level of grace and character unmatched by any other American icon. With undeniable poise, Jackie rode through scandal after scandal, the obvious infidelities of her husband and his eventual assassination while maintaining a strength through which she could continue to parent her children in the public eye. In a position that would defeat most women, Jackie rose above the challenges and proved to the world that she was a true Bombshell.

The tragedies that befell the Kennedy family would only multiply, including the sudden disappearance and presumed death of her son, John F. Kennedy, Jr. There is one thing that can't go without saying: only a woman of extreme spirit and substance would be able to emerge from this cruel and profound sadness without losing herself in pity. It would have been so easy for her to engage in self-destructive behaviour—not that the world wouldn't have understood why.

Jacqueline was tested repeatedly by life but also took it upon herself to test life by taking the chance to love and live again in a world that had been unkind to her. She was a Bombshell success, never allowing herself to lose sight of the gifts and strength she possessed and never losing her graceful disposition. Jackie's ability to acknowledge and celebrate her gifts as a woman afforded her the clear-headedness to choose a winning life team, a support network fueled by sharing her soul.

The difference between this Bombshell and other women of her time is that Jackie refused to make excuses for failure. She demonstrated to her children and to women across the world that it was possible to fall back on the power and strength that she had nurtured throughout her life even in the face of crushing adversity. When some of the most precious things in life had been taken from her, Jackie O. knew that her gifts were going to carry her through even when many said she would always endure the "Kennedy curse." She died not only a true Bombshell, but a timeless inspiration.

Madonna: Not Just a Material Girl

Few women in Hollywood have been able to achieve true Bombshell status but Madonna is a perfect example of the successful modern-day Bombshell. In every aspect of her career she has managed to peel away different layers of herself as a woman, constantly uncovering fantastic new elements of herself to share with the world while still embracing all past aspects of herself. Madonna knows her strengths and makes the most of them. In return she has achieved a carefully orchestrated life of power and success. She has proven herself timeless, which can be extremely difficult to achieve in the world of popular music as fans can be fickle. The public demands performers to remain musically, socially and physically evolved at all times. This is no easy task.

Madonna managed to transform the world of fashion early on in her career. She created new and unique fashion trends on a regular basis and was totally unapologetic when shocking the faint of heart. She constantly transcends the former with something even more popular and unusual. The world has watched intently as each album has become a smash-hit. Some thought she would fade into aging pop star status, while others believed she might have an Elvis-style meltdown and fade to black. How wrong they were. The sparkle of Madonna's strength is only gaining momentum and the love and adoration of her fans gives her the inspiration to continue to influence women of the world to gather their own strength and find their own ways to shine.

In recent years a new and equally successful dimension to Madonna's life has been added: motherhood. Many were unable to picture this ultra-sexy, glamorous, outspoken woman as a loving and nurturing mother. However, as any Bombshell knows, one of these traits is not necessarily mutually exclusive of the other. So, fulfilling the role of a lifetime, Madonna seems to have shown the world her endless sparkle and strength. In true Bombshell-style, this icon makes no apologies for her power and strength as the truly unique individual she continues to be and we can only hope she is passing this down to the "mini Bombshells" she has been gifted with!

Oprah: The One Woman Show

Seldom has a woman touched so many with the generosity and kindness displayed by Oprah Winfrey. One of my personal mentors and a Bombshell in the truest sense, she has shown the world the power of grace and self acceptance unparalleled by any other woman in this century.

Born in Mississippi in the mid-50s, this soon to be mega-Bombshell would not only overcome the challenges facing a female African American during a time when society had not yet evolved to embracing all colors, creeds and sexes as equal, (though we still have far to go) she would exceed all expectations. Mississippi was perhaps not the friendliest of places for a young girl born out of wedlock and into severe poverty; clearly this young woman would have to take control of her destiny in order to overcome what some would see as insurmountable social and economic hurdles. The young Oprah eventually moved to Milwaukee with the hope of better opportunity, but this provided only more devastating and almost tragic circumstances for her.

Repeatedly sexually abused as a young girl and having had bouts of out-right wild child behavior, the resilient and spirited Oprah fought still to find her inner Bombshell and become something better than what was expected of her during those times. Illustrating the power of choice, Oprah moved again, this time to be with her father. Oprah's father was a strict and structured force in her life and very soon she was on the path to achieving what many only dream of.

After attending university at Tennessee State this rising star held television anchor positions never before held by a black woman and Oprah's unstoppable talent was emerging, fueled by her spirit and determination to succeed.

In 1984 Oprah took a job hosting a morning talk show in a competing time slot with the Phil Donahue show, a serious risk that would eventually pay off. She showed yet another element of her talent as a performer when she starred in the 1985 movie, The Color Purple, giving a moving and unforgettable performance by a gifted woman that the world would soon come to view as one of the most influential of our time.

The success of Oprah's talk show career comes not with the format or the marketing of her program, as these have all been done before. Her success in this arena comes from the obvious personal struggles that she has chosen to share with the world, making all women feel as though she is just a little bit like them and making no apologies for her tenacity. Being so willing to show her vulnerabilities in a Hollywood world of "pretend to be perfect" makes Oprah the most sparkling kind of Bombshell. It is the embracing and sharing of her weight issues that reinforced to women of the world that we are all fighting for something but that the true beauty of a woman can be housed in a size 22 as well as a model body of size 4.

Arguably the most powerful woman in the world and not just by the numbers of her enormous income but by the number of lives she has changed over the decades, Oprah continues to remind women to accept the flaws they feel they have in order to lessen the power they have over us. She has been willing to bare her soul to the world, inspiring and even compelling us to show our inner Bombshell and choose success for ourselves. A consummate leader for women of the world not limited by heritage or status, Oprah has the found her true and steadfast inner Bombshell but more importantly has chosen to share it with the entire world.

CHAPTER TWO

From Boredom to Bombshell

CHAPTER TWO
From Boredom to Bombshell

T he Bombshell will soon learn that the smallest things can boost her sparkle and increase her self-confidence exponentially. This is never a vain attempt to become a vision of perfection; it is about embracing our beauty, flaws and all! The teachings of the following chapters are more about the everyday ways to bring out your own special and unique Bombshell qualities in ways that make you feel most confident. Keeping up with the times is essential, but personalizing these things with your own unique touches is equally as important. The glitter from your soul's beauty will be free-flowing when given the right canvas from which to spring!

One key element to keeping all of the beauty information you are about to learn in order is to keep a Beauty File. In here you can keep pictures, ideas and informational notes on techniques, colors and anything else you might find helpful so that it will be available for your reference at the quickest glance. So get yours ready—it will fill up faster than you think!

Hair

Okay, we must admit that there is a reason the term "bad hair day" is known to women all over the world. Hair plays a large role in the determination of one's level of confidence; a really great hair day can make your mood, but a bad hair day can just as easily sink it. Let's face it, when your hair is great, you walk a little taller, smile a little wider and even the sky can look a little brighter. So take a good look at the way your hair is styled, and I don't mean out of the gym or first thing in the morning, but as you would style it on an average day. If it doesn't make you feel a little sparkly and feminine then we need to "tawk!" Who do you think has great hair? Look into ways that you can modify this style to suit your face, body and skin. Cut out pictures from magazines and take them to your stylist, or try consulting with a new stylist, as most salons offer this consultation free of charge. It can often be that these are offered with some of their newest talent but don't worry, often these junior stylists have fresher, edgier ideas and techniques and who knows, you just might find a great talent. Besides, you are only getting a consultation, not handing them the scissors. If you don't like the direction they're going, thank them and tell them you are thinking about it!

> **Tip:** Don't go into the salon and ask for the most expensive stylist. Just because this person has seniority doesn't mean they would handle your hair type best. Ask the person at the booking desk to recommend the stylist who would best suit your hair type and length.

Remember that a large factor in becoming the Bombshell that you know you can be is keeping your look fresh and updated while still feeling like yourself. Ultra-trendy hair can be fun once in a while, but remember to try and modify the shape a little bit so that you are not sharing the same hairstyle as the rest of the world.

Once you have found the haircut and stylist that best suit you, you will discover that you have won a big part of the hair battle—but it's not over yet! There is a great temptation to sit back while your hair is being styled and dried, but this is definitely not the time to zone out. This is actually a very good time to learn styling techniques to use at home. You are paying your stylist to do the work, so why not get a free lesson in your own hair care while you are at it? Take note of the products being used in your hair and don't be afraid to ask questions about them and why they work with your hair type. Where does your stylist start to blow dry your hair and how are they holding the dryer? Pay attention to details like these and even take notes if you are not going to be back in that chair for a while. After trying it yourself a few times you will get the technique down and love the results you see even by doing it at home!

> **Tip:** Don't get pushed into leaving the salon having spent a fortune in products, but do make sure to invest in a great conditioner More often than not you can get away with a cheaper shampoo but a great conditioner will really affect your finished hairstyle. Remember, you don't have to use expensive products everyday; you can alternate their use. Or, for salon-quality products at a reduced cost, try shopping at beauty supply shops.

Hair Color

It is now time to assess the color of your hair. Is it looking a little washed out, faded or generally less flattering than it might be? If you have been coloring your hair with drug store dyes without having so much as a salon consultation, then I must tell you that it's worth the time to go and get this done. Even if you don't get the color done then and there, it is a good education on what you may ultimately want to achieve. You will rarely find a good colorist in the person who cuts your hair, but don't rule out this possibility entirely. The same rules apply when you are looking for a colorist as they did for a stylist: cut out photos and bring them in, but be flexible in color and tone so that you can get the best advice on what suits you best. Remember that not everyone suits platinum blonde or fire engine red!

Once you have found a color technician that you feel confident with, it is time to look at color charts. See what your professional recommends and guide them with your own ideas and preferences. When you come to an agreement on a shade, write it down and put it in your Beauty File. Never let yourself be pushed into something you are not keen on because ultimately you may not feel comfortable with the result and this will undermine your self-confidence. Anyone you are paying for a service is technically working for you, so speak your mind and see if you can strike the perfect balance between what you would like and what the professional advises. If you have done your research you should be able to find a colorist who you can really communicate well with and who gives you honest, helpful advice on what looks can successfully be achieved with your hair.

So are you thrilled with the outcome of your hair? Good! If not, remember that color can be modified with highlights and lowlights; so don't panic. Now it is time to address the upkeep of your new hair color! If you have gone from darker hair to a lighter shade, you must not let your roots get ahead of you—no matter what Madonna may be doing these days. I realize that this may seem to be a very expensive proposition, but there are ways to get around enormous costs. As soon as you get your new color down, find out who makes it and what the color number is. You should do this for several reasons: hairstylists tend to move frequently and usually take their files with them—and the Bombshell does not want to be left stranded! Also, once you know the manufacturer and color, you can call beauty supply stores to see if they carry the color for you to do touch-ups yourself.

The only color process I would caution against doing at home is one that involves any kind of bleaching; every other color can be done on your own—just watch your colorist next time and see how it is done properly. By using the right professional products and applicator brushes you should be able to cut those salon colorings in half while maintaining an immaculate, professional-looking appearance. If you cannot find the exact color, then start visiting beauty supply stores and ask to see their color charts. The staff at these stores should be able to help you pick out a base color that is close to what you have and be able to tell you how to mix it properly. If you are not ready to do this yourself, then keep watching your color technician and learn the finer points of the process. While you are at the beauty supply store, look for the good hair brushes and products that your stylist uses as they are generally priced at a reduced rate here. Better still, if you happen to know any stylists personally, you can get products at wholesale prices—but make sure to do this on the QT.

Now you must be wondering how on earth you are supposed to color the back of your head on your own. This is where you get by with a little help from your friends! I have a great group of female friends, who after deciding to make the transition from barely noticeable to true Bombshell, have become members of the monthly "Wine and Roots Club." Now some of these women could easily afford the $65 to $100+ every couple of weeks but find the ritual a great time to share each other's company and shopping tips. By doing every other hair color yourself, you can save up to $600 a year—major shoe money!

Now that you have the cut and color you love, my final piece of advice is to always take that extra half an hour for yourself. I know that this isn't always easy, as many of us are wives, mothers and businesswomen, but it is important. Always keep in mind that along with all of those roles, you are still a woman and there should never be guilt for investing in yourself and being the very best that you can be. That extra time on your hair can really add up to a better day or more opportunity as a result of feeling that extra bit of confidence.

Make-up

I could actually hear you groan when you read those little words, but don't be scared. It is so much easier that you think; you just have to have fun with it! Make-up can be so important to women—even if it looks like you aren't wearing any at all. When you look at yourself in the mirror, what do you think of your face? Make a list of the things that really bother you and study yourself for the things you really like. Do you have great skin? Full lips? High cheekbones? A cute nose? Remember that make-up is about enhancing and drawing attention to the features that you feel are your best, while helping distract from and minimize the things that you really don't like.

The first thing I suggest is going through all of your make-up and getting rid of anything that is broken, dried out, expired or just generally makes you gasp. So, do you have anything left? The next step is to book a few afternoons to go to department stores in your area and check out the make-up counters. Many people find the cosmetics section to be a little intimidating, but remember that the people in these places have been put there to help you—just ask. Try a couple of different counters every trip (all in one day would be too overwhelming) and book the free consultations and make-up applications that almost every make-up manufacturer offers. Often the people at these counters will have time to see you on the spot (especially if you go on a particularly idle Tuesday afternoon), so you may as well take advantage of it. Many of the staff here are trained and experienced make-up artists who are eager to show off their talents. A little praise and genuine appreciation for their craft will go a long way toward some free samples and that extra special attention afforded to all Bombshells!

Try and have some ideas in mind for yourself. Remember the list of things that you would like to focus on and tell the make-up artist so that you two are on the same page. It may be a good idea to take a few pictures from your Beauty File to discuss with the make-up artist. Show them what you like about the photos and ask them how they would recommend going about achieving these looks for you. Also tell them what looks you dislike so they will know not to try them on you. I think I should warn you that some of these make-up jobs will scare you no matter how beautiful you are, but your look is only a washcloth away from repair. Not everyone at these kiosks knows what they are doing, so just keep trying new ones. Don't forget to take notes on particular colors and styles that you really love and if possible, watch the make-up artist in the mirror as they do your application so that you learn brush strokes and some of the tricks essential to highlighting your eyes, cheeks and lips. Put all of this information into your Beauty File when you get home so that you can refer to it when you are next inspired to try a new look. When you go for these make-up applications, make sure to get a mix of day looks and evening options—this can be particularly fun if you book it just before a girls' night out. Nighttime make-up is often darker, more fun and affords you a little more creative flexibility once you know what you are doing.

Don't think for a minute that these people aren't going to try to sell you every product they used on you. Especially beware of this if you are at the Chanel or Dior counter where a new line of make-up can cost you more than a car payment. If you have the money to spend and love a certain product, then go ahead and splurge, but only after having comparison shopped at other kiosks and the drug store to make sure that you are treating yourself to the right one. Don't be afraid to tell the salesperson that you are trying out several new products before you make your decision. Remember that many of the "designer" make-up companies, like Clinique, Lancôme, Prescriptives and others could be subsidiaries of either L'Oreal or Estée Lauder and that as a result, the drug store equivalent of what you would buy in a department store is of a similar quality at a lower price point. And yes, I did just say drug store. Drug store make-up is no longer the faux pas it once was. For example, I once paid $30 for mascara at a high end department store and found that the $6 one I got from the drug store actually worked better for my lashes. Let this be a lesson: do not let the price of the product fool you. Also, don't forget to keep your receipt until you know that you love the product. Many of us buy something that we soon find will not work for us in color or style and then we end up tossing it into the abyss that is the bathroom drawer thinking that we should have known better. To this I say: return, return, return! If you are not satisfied with a product you can take it back (as long as it is not half used, of course). There is no reason to incur expenses for products that you are not happy with.

Armed with your notes on colors and styles of make-up application, it is now time to start purchasing your essentials. What are the essentials, you ask? *Here is a list of suggested minimum requirements:*
- a good foundation
- a fantastic powder

- blush
- several different shadows in your complimentary colors
- mascara (one regular, one waterproof)
- liners for both the lips and the eyes
- a few different lipsticks (day and night colors) and lip gloss to match

Tip: Once you find the colors you really love start cruising the drug store aisles for a similar shade and try it out. You can often get the same effect at a much lower price.

I always find that mixing certain expensive products with others that are less costly can produce the exact same Bombshell look as it would if I had spent a fortune on strictly expensive make-up, so try mixing it up.

Remember that you don't always have to wear full make-up, but you will likely want to wear a little just so it shows that you have taken the time for yourself. When you spend that extra three minutes on a gentle swipe of mascara and lip gloss you will invariably feel one hundred percent better about yourself, and this will be felt by those around you. Never forget that the way you feel about yourself projects out onto all those you come into contact with . . . sometimes a little lip shine helps a little soul shine!

Now if there is one thing to invest money in when it comes to make-up it is a set of good brushes and applicators: you will only be as good as the tools you have to work with. Have you ever tried painting a house with a cheap brush? It's a nightmare. Do not skimp on your brushes as it will make professional-looking make-up more difficult to achieve. I recommend taking your notes on the applicators you liked best in the mini-makeovers and get the appropriate equivalents.

Tip: Look for brush sets as this is often the only way to save on make-up applicators. Make sure that you like and will use most of the brushes in the set or you will not really be getting a deal. Holiday time is often a great time to find these sets.

Let the salesperson show you the best ways to use the individual brushes and don't feel strange if all of your brushes are from different companies because some make better brushes for different uses than others. For some, the best thing is to buy one pricey brush at a time to build your collection less painfully. If you take good care of your brushes, they can last you for years (Heck, that's longer than some of the men I've had!).

Wash your brushes in a gentle baby shampoo every so often and lay them on a cloth to air dry to save yourself the expense of having to buy a special brush cleaner.

Keep in mind that the whole make-up process can be really fun and relaxing once you get some professional advice. When you find (or make) the time, then start to practice every chance you get. I do not recommend trying a new look the evening of an important event, but if you have been taking the time for yourself, you should be prepared to throw on a face whenever necessary. If you have young children and find that they are all over you the minute you sit down to do your make-up, set them up with all of your old palettes and cheap brushes so they can do their own make-up right beside you. Even little boys can get into the act if you suggest they do themselves up like an action hero!

Hairy Lips and Lawn Maintenance

This may scare you but go out and get yourself the strongest magnifying mirror you can find because the right tools here will make your life so much easier. I recommend a magnification of at least seven times or stronger. Usually these mirrors are free-standing and have one side that is a regular magnification and the other to prove that those things you thought were fallen eyelashes are actually the chin whiskers you've heard your mother talking about! Chances are that if you are over the age of twenty-five you will have a few of these little beauties somewhere on your face. Now for the next tool: a pair of fantastic, never-fail-to-get-the-little-suckers tweezers. Tweezerman are the best ones I have found so far and I keep several pairs on hand in case I go traveling or the kids get their hands on them for their next arts and crafts project! Once you get a good look in the magnifying mirror, I suspect you will see the need for eyebrow and perhaps other facial waxing or hair removal. Bombshells avoid wearing moustaches at all costs, regardless of what Janet Reno thinks is sexy.

Waxing and other forms of hair removal have been around for ages and there is good reason for this: property value goes way up with landscaping. From head to toe, lawn maintenance is essential. Waxing or plucking the eyebrows can open the eye and update your look immediately and at a minimal cost.

I recommend getting a good eyebrow shaping every other month with a recommended professional and then maintain it yourself in between visits with your powerful mirror and good tweezers. Avoid over-plucking or waxing because a super-thin brow often looks harsh and can cause you to have an angry look on an otherwise pretty and friendly face.

So you never thought that you would have lip- or chin-fuzz but upon further inspection discover you do? Well, the truth of the matter is that it has to go. I am not talking about the blondish fuzz that we all have, but anything with a darker coloring definitely needs to be taken care of. There are many ways to do this, but waxing seems to be the most economical, long-lasting way to get rid of this unsightly hair quickly. Your choice in aesthetician should be made very carefully because this is your face we are talking about. Ask your friends and family if they know anyone who they might recommend, someone who is good at what they do and can do it as painlessly as possible. Laser hair removal is also a great option but it comes at a substantial cost.

The Hair Down There

Not to get too personal, but bikini maintenance is very important. You want to feel put together from head to toe, so why not consider landscaping everywhere? In this region you have the option to shave—you weren't considering this for your face, were you? Shaving is painless, effective and easy to do. The rule here is that anything outside of your normal bathing suit region should be completely smooth.

And don't forget that hairstyles change over the years Bombshell, including that feminine bush you've been sporting since 1981. Trim that thing, would you? You'll thank me later. Even this kind of update can make you feel a little younger and more fashionable even though you may be the only one who sees it!

Speaking of hair on womanly bits, hairy nipples are wrong . . . unless of course your knuckles are still scraping the ground! Sounds obvious to some but other Bombshells in training are perhaps a little sheltered from the ways of feminine landscape and design. Take whatever steps you feel comfortable with when achieving this goal just make sure to maintain it and look in a good mirror for any strays below the nipple line!

Tip: Most beauty supply stores sell professional waxing pots and equipment that can be great to have at home as long as you are not squeamish. If you buy one, get advice on which waxes work best with which applicators and pre-wax cleansers, as these are vitally important. This can also be a joint venture between you and some close friends. Split the cost and wax each other! Just make sure you have all had it done enough to know what to do and keep an eye on the wax temperature so that no one gets burned. For the truly brazen Bombshell, try a Brazilian— but this should only be done by someone with experience and (I suspect) a good glass of wine!

One last thing about hair removal: look in the spots you normally wouldn't concentrate on, like the backs of your knees and thighs and whatever you do, look at your toes! It will only take an extra few seconds to de-fuzz the little beauties and it adds to the image of impeccable care of you and your parts.

Hands and Feet

Did you know that when surveyed, almost all men noted a woman's hands or feet as a determining factor in their perception of the way she takes care of herself? Make no mistake, a Bombshell is a Bombshell for herself, but being attractive to the opposite sex seems like a pretty good side effect to me! Whether you have short or long nails (but maybe not Flo-Jo long), keep them well-maintained. This will be a strong visual indication that you care about yourself and pay attention to detail. While this may not seem important to you, it speaks volumes about you in everything from job interviews to dates. I am not advocating getting manicures and pedicures everyday, although in a perfect world we all could; there are tons of small, independent nail salons that have competitive prices and you can often get a mani/pedi for around $40. Another option is the acrylic nail. Long or short, these are incredibly durable and more economical than ever to fill and shape as they grow.

The cost of maintaining one's hands and feet has come down so drastically over time that I don't even recommend trying it yourself as you will spend huge amounts of time and not save much financially in the end.

You should, however, make sure that the salon you choose follows the current health regulations and that it looks clean and well-kept upon visual inspection.

Now for the feet! Are you one of those "only when I go away" or "I just can't be bothered" people? Well, we'll be having no more of that. Your feet should be pretty at all times, even if you are just doing home pedis and applying a clear polish; though I really think that for the cost, it is worth it to take the hour for yourself and get them done professionally. This can be a great time to take a breather and totally relax. Many salons are capable of doing your hands and feet at the same time, so you can be in and out in no time! I recommend taking your own polish so that you can do any color touch-ups at home as toes can chip long before you need another pedicure and chipped polish is a big Bombshell faux pas. Don't forget that all of these things are investments in you as a woman. The happier you are, the better mother, lover or businesswoman you will become.

Try a few of these spa-like treatments at home to prolong pretty hands and feet; they really work and will save you money. Take all of the half-bottles of face, hand or body lotions you have; combine them; add some vitamin E oil; give it a shake and keep it for your home hand and foot treatments. Slather your hands and feet and cover them in plastic wrap while you watch TV or read a book. You can also sleep with this on to penetrate deeper into your skin. You will be amazed at the difference in the health of your skin after a few moisturizing wraps. All of the steps we take in looking after ourselves go a long way towards repairing the daily stresses we impose on our bodies and gives us the extra encouragement we may sometimes need to pursue our goals.

If you are ever in doubt about the changing trends of the female landscape then go out and buy yourself a Playboy magazine. I'm not suggesting you buy it from the local store or where you take your kids for ice cream in the summer, but you can go elsewhere and grab one. This can be like a fashion magazine for your womanly bits and may save you the embarrassing water cooler questions like "So, do you trim or wax?" Do not, for a moment, think that your body has to look like these women's (okay, girls really) but it is a good resource for styles that you may want to explore.

Well, I think I have covered head to toe and in between pretty well. Keep in mind that this self-assessment is for you and your Beauty File only. Don't ever compare yourself to anyone else; the only yardstick worth measuring against is your own. Keeping an account of your beauty evolution will amaze you, so keep pictures of your progress to remind yourself of what it is that you are striving for and how far you have come. You will see the changes in your eyes, and you will start to feel them in your heart, I promise.

"I don't care if you do lunges all the way home from the kids bus stop, just do them!"

"The better you look going to the gym can actually help get you there"

"We should get a hero bisquit after giving birth but we usually just get stretch marks!"

"A dimmer switch is a great way to lose 10lbs!"

CHAPTER THREE

Working Up to Working Out

CHAPTER THREE
Working Up to Working Out

O kay, I confess that I am no guru when it comes to exercise (he comes later in this chapter). Let's face it; I am a Bombshell, not a bodybuilder! I'm not saying it is impossible to be both, but generally Bombshells don't go to these kinds of extremes. On a more serious note, there are hundreds of reasons and thousands of studies to promote the importance of physical fitness for women (and men, too). We know for certain that those who are active live longer, have more energy and are, for the most part, more alert, attractive people. Also, we know that even a moderate workout can trigger the release of healthy, mood enhancing hormones and help us avoid giving off that "if you even look at me sideways I will hurt you" energy. Sign me up for a dose of the good ones!

I know that working out can be a daunting task, but it is time to look around your neighborhood for different fitness facilities. I believe that the buddy system works best when it comes to exercise for several reasons. Firstly, it is always good to get input from a friend, and secondly, you will have someone to go for a martini lunch with to celebrate your new found Mecca of sweat and tears.

Bombshell, it is important to remember a few key factors in choosing a workout environment. Not only are a clean and relaxed, low stress space necessary, but so is a close proximity to a good spa! Seriously though, you need to be able to walk into the place and feel at ease. If you see a room full of free weights and juice-shooting muscleheads, you are probably in the wrong place.

Once you have decided where you (and hopefully a few good friends) will be working out, it is time to negotiate membership fees. Remember that spending a fortune for a gym is almost always unnecessary as many smaller, less expensive gyms will have exactly what you need without going over the top. There is a lot of competition out there, so make sure to keep that in mind. If there are several of you signing up at the same time, you should be able to get a reduced rate, like a corporate rate, or waived initiation fees.

Most good fitness clubs will give you an orientation to the club with a personal trainer. Be sure to take advantage of this as it will allow you to learn how the different machines work and how to do the exercises properly. Every exercise that you do correctly will be worth ten done incorrectly, so take full advantage of your time with the trainer. Make a list of all the questions you might have beforehand and don't feel silly asking them because they are professionals and the right people to be answering them. There is nothing worse than wandering aimlessly through a gym. Feeling intimidated at first is natural, but with a little research and a few questions you can alleviate a lot of the stress associated with starting a new workout regime. Try picking up a few fitness magazines to learn some of the lingo as well as getting tips on nutrition and healthy eating.

Included in your membership package should be the formulation of your personalized workout routine. The trainer should ask you what your goals are and help you put together the best plan for you to reach your target. This would be a good time to take a few "before" pictures to keep in your Beauty File. They are for no one else to see but will serve to encourage you to continue once you start to see the physical changes happening. Don't be too critical of yourself as the whole point of this is to focus on the wonderful qualities you already possess.

Getting into the habit of exercising three or four times a week (or as many as you can) won't be the easiest thing you have ever done, but in time you will find it to be one of the most rewarding. Do not stop once you start! That very precious momentum can be easily lost but is exceptionally hard to regain. In a matter of weeks you will start to look and feel better than you ever thought possible. The time you take for your physical fitness will afford you strength of mind in addition to strength in body. Anything that gives you that feeling of accomplishment is a good building block for healthy self-esteem—one of the Bombshell's essential characteristics.

Some days will feel better than others, but don't beat yourself up for missing a day or even a week at the gym; even the Bombshell needs a vacation! Do make sure to get right back on track and in no time you will have paid the calorie gods for those extra few glasses of champagne. You will find the motivation of friends to be invaluable, especially on the days that you don't feel like trekking to the gym. And if money is no object, or if you choose to organize your financial priorities to suit this, then book sessions with a trainer from your gym to give you that extra incentive to show up!

When you go to the gym, go looking good. I am not saying that you should go in full hair and make-up, but certainly make an effort to go looking well kept and attractive because believe it or not, when you walk past the wall-length mirror and feel good, you will likely give yourself the extra assurance required to boost your workout to a higher level. Something as seemingly unimportant as what you wear to exercise in can make a noticeable difference in your performance. Looking the part can play a huge role in putting you in the frame of mind to achieve your fitness goals. Get yourself two great workout outfits (with mixing and matching they become four!) that make you feel good to exercise in and that you love; I promise this will help. If you look forward to wearing these outfits, you will be more likely to workout when you want and will feel better as you do so. And of course, make sure that you have shoes that not only fit your feet properly, but that are also suited to the type of exercise you are doing. Be sure to ask questions and provide important information to the person helping you choose your next pair of running shoes.

Tip: Don't buy products from the gym boutique as they tend to be more expensive than others. Get last year's style in running shoe; they are still good shoes, just a different design. Also, try different off-price retail chains like Winners or Ross' for great workout wear at a fraction of the price of other retail stores.

Now, if you don't have space in your budget to join a gym, there are many ways for you to workout at home. But, remember that working out at home requires a stronger motivation and more discipline on your part as it is easy to slack off or skip a workout all together. If you don't have a friend to join you in home workouts, I suggest setting all of the alarm clocks in your house for the same time so that when they all start screaming at you, you will be motivated enough to turn them off one by one and maybe even be enticed to start your workout. There are also some great exercise videos available, but you won't see results only if you use them as paperweights! If videos are not your style, get a skipping rope and go outside or into the basement for short sessions of skipping a few times during the day.

As I stated earlier, I am no fitness expert. I did, however, manage to bring one in for all those who read this chapter and become truly inspired to find the healthier, stronger Bombshell lurking within!

Larry Track has devised some really wonderful and simple plans to help with your fitness transformation. Remember Bombshell, if you have no previous experience with exercise or don't really know how to do something properly make sure you get advice to help you achieve the desired form. An injured Bombshell is not the goal here!

Getting on Track at Home: the Full Body Three-Minute Drill

There are so many options for working out. Not all of them require a gym membership. Perhaps all you need is to go for a brisk walk with some of your neighbors a couple of times a week. Whatever it is that you decide on, make sure you stick with it because that is the only way you will see results.

Here is a suggested exercise program from personal trainer and fitness guru Larry Track that is suitable for every Bombshell to do from the privacy of her own home. This program has been designed to only take three minutes of your day at home with no equipment. It will leave you feeling fantastic and fit. We all have three minutes for fitness!

Beginners:　　Use 500ml water bottles as your weights
　　　　　　　(these weigh 1lb. each)

Intermediate:　Use 1.5L water bottles as your weights
　　　　　　　(these weigh 3.3lbs. each)

Advanced:　　Use 5lb. weights

Phase 1: Muscle Group Wake Up Call

Day One: Legs and Abs

- Squat—20 reps
- Dead-lifts—20 reps
- Step-ups—20 reps
- Standing calf raises—20 reps
- Walking lunges—10 lunges on each leg
- Crunch—20 reps
- Reverse crunch—20 reps

Day Two: Chest and Abs

- Cross body punches—50 reps
- Push-ups—Max (do as many as you can)
- Repeat the above two exercises for 3 rounds
- Lying pelvic tilt—20 reps
- Crunch—20 reps
- Lying pelvic tilt—20 reps
- Crunch—20 reps

Day Three: Shoulders and Abs

- Shoulder press—20 reps
- Crunch—20 reps
- Front raise—20 reps
- Crunch—20 reps
- Lateral raise—20 reps
- Crunch—20 reps
- Jumping jacks—30 reps

Day Four: Back and Abs

- Bent over rear delt flys—20 reps
- Bent over rows—20 reps
- Push-ups—10 reps
- Repeat for 2 rounds
- 20 crunches
- 20 reverse crunch

Day Five: Arms and Abs

- Hammer curl (just like you would grip a hammer)—20 reps
- Tricep kickbacks—20 reps
- Crunch—20 reps
- Bicep curl—20 reps
- One arm overhead extensions—10 each arm
- Scissor crunch—10 reps each leg
- Crunch—20 reps

Day Six: Full body

- Squat—21 reps
- Bicep curl—21 reps
- Shoulder press—21 reps
- Bent over rows—11 reps on each arm
- Push-ups—21 reps
  (do as many as you can from your toes then fall to your knees if needed to complete)
- Dips—21reps
- Crunch—30 reps

Day 7: Off

Phase 2: The Daily Full Body Track Attack

Day 1: Star

- Dips—15 reps
- Bicep curls—20 reps
- Bent over rows—30 reps
- Squat—40 reps
- Crunch—50 reps
- Jumping jacks—60 reps
- Cross-body punches—100 reps

Day 2: Runway

- Crunch—10 reps
- Squat static hold (hold squat position, don't move!)—30 seconds
- Reverse crunch—10 reps
- Push-ups—10 reps
- Scissor crunch—15 each leg
- Dips—10 reps
- Pelvic tilt—10 reps
- Front raise—10 reps
- Cross-over crunch—15 each way (30 total)
- Dead-lifts—10 reps

Day 3: Vogue

- Step-ups—10 reps each leg
- Push-ups—20 reps
- Shoulder press—20 reps
- Hammer curl—20 reps
- Tricep kickbacks—20 reps
- Reverse crunch—30 reps

Day 4: Jeans

- Lunge—10 reps each leg
- Walking on the spot (lift each knee 15 times)
- Step-ups—10 each leg
- Repeat for 2 total rounds
- Squat—50 reps
- Crunch—30 reps

Day 5: Saturday Night

- Jumping jacks—30 reps
- Push-ups—20 reps
- Jumping jacks—30 reps
- Lateral raise—20 reps
- Jumping jacks—30 reps
- Squat—20 reps
- Pelvic tilt—20 reps
- Crunch—20 reps

Day 6: Beach

- Squat—1 minute
- Push-ups—5 reps
- Squat—1 minute
- Push-ups—5 reps
- Crunch—30 reps

Day 7: Off

Now you have no excuse to get started. It's time to work out Bombshell-style! At home, at the gym, or for the very lucky Bombshell, at a private facility, this kind of change can only support your healthy and happy Bombshell outlook.

"Smiling is a silent hello that screams Bombshell"

"A genuine laugh is the most powerful and infectious sound, it is almost the mating call of a true Bombshell...even when she's laughing at herself"

"There is a reason that magic wands have light and sparkle...the magic wand of a Bombshell is the touch of her hand"

CHAPTER FOUR

Smiling—The Super Easy Superpower

CHAPTER FOUR
Smiling—The Super Easy Superpower

D id you know that one of the most attractive things about a person is the openness conveyed by the warmth of their smile? It's true. If you start to notice all of the people you pass by on a daily basis you will start to see how few women appear to be kind and approachable. This is precisely why the Bombshell wants to make a concerted effort to display her happiness at all times. I know that this sounds serious but I am convinced that it takes more of an effort to maintain the poker face that society has deemed to be the mask of safety. There is no faster or more effective way to become beautiful than sporting a genuine smile. Even just reminding yourself to keep a friendly look on your face will impart that sense of warmth to others.

The Bombshell has a great number of things to be thankful for and needs to convey this sense of good fortune to all. The next time you go shopping or to a sporting event, take a look around you. Is it possible that all of the sullen and blank looks you see on people's faces are legitimate, or do these people really have things to be happy about? Imagine being the one person in the sea of mediocrity that surrounds you who shows her true feelings on her face and truly shines as a result. This is what will set you apart from the crowd dear Bombshell, so why not be the one who walks around feeling her own positive energy and sharing it with others?

There is a certain amount of mystery behind the woman who walks into the room with a glowing smile. Passers-by will stop to get a closer look in the hopes that they can discover what you have to be so happy about. There are many different looks you can send out and I don't think walking around like you just spent the night with George Clooney is always the most appropriate; but hey, even that has its place!

Often in social situations women try too hard to look confident and they end up looking smug and unapproachable. This is such a big mistake and is one that we Bombshells avoid at all costs. I have seen some incredibly beautiful women wearing veils of insecurity and it really hid the glow that would otherwise come naturally from them. There is also a misconception that powerful or influential men are looking for women that are a challenge and that looking slightly aloof is a good strategy to attract a man of this quality. Do not buy into this as it will only serve to hide your wonderful, shining self and Mr. Right will be far more likely to pass you by simply because you stifled your sparkle. Also, it doesn't matter how powerful or intelligent a man may be, he won't be interested in setting himself up for rejection and when you give off a sour air, he won't be interested in searching out the sweetness that lurks underneath. Smile at everyone; it really is okay and will only serve as a great tool for you to convey the happiness you are capable of spreading to others.

Does all of this seem like too much work for you dear Bombshell? Then you might need to go back and re-master a few of the previous steps because once you start to see yourself becoming a sparkly being you will automatically look happy and relaxed. It's funny, but for some women the smile is the hardest thing to master. I surmise that for many women the possibility of "smile rejection" is too great a risk; you must be confident that this will not be an issue for the true Bombshell—she doesn't look happy and smile just to get this in return, she does it because she is deeply satisfied with herself. Not being afraid to show this and share it with all who embrace this gift is both liberating and empowering to you as a woman. The smile is your way of expressing your own personal contentment. I don't even notice if people smile back because I'm not using my warmth as currency in order to acquire something; my smile is a statement of my own level of self-acceptance and my readiness to embrace others.

Still scared to walk around with that knowing smile on your face?

> **Try This:** Go for a walk and begin smiling at babies and children. Don't go running after new moms or anything, but whenever you pass young children and babies, take a moment to notice what happens when you smile at them. What you will notice is truly remarkable; they are visibly drawn to you and their faces and actions will light up when you engage them in your warmth.

Now what makes us think that we ever lose that basic human attraction to a warm and gentle face? Take full advantage of the things that are most powerful and basic when perfecting your Bombshell skills as the things that are so inherently human are the specialties of any true Bombshell.

Smiling and Its Corporate Power

I have been in a few business meetings in my time and am always amazed at how many people check their smile at the door along with their umbrella! Keeping in mind that the "village idiot" look isn't what you are going for, let's explore the application of a great smile to successful negotiations.

I'm sure that there are many people who subscribe to the notion that to be strong and competent, you have to look tough. This might be true if you are a wrestler but for the average person there is no rule that says you have to give up appearing friendly in order to achieve success in business and your career. A Bombshell is always able to find the balance between smart and ambitious, tempering this with her innate ability to smile and persuade. Let's face it, when it comes to negotiations, there is no one better than the Bombshell! You see, sometimes people need to be disarmed a little so that they will be more likely to make the odd concession, thereby making it much easier to come to a mutual agreement with you. Every person on the planet would rather deal with someone who has a friendly, non-threatening manner than an overly aggressive personality. My mother always used to say, "Jacqueline darling, you will always get more with honey than you do with vinegar." How true this has proven to be! Although, I should warn you that every once in a while a girl has to dig in her high heels and be ready for a bit of a battle, but believe me, you will win the war when you go in Bombshell-style!

Sometimes the smile is just what it takes to bring business situations down to a more human level, so instead of pitting yourself against someone, you are able to convey a sense of camaraderie just by smiling and showing that you possess an open, friendly attitude. You have such a powerful tool at the tip of your tongue; a silent, disarming charm that can be exactly what you need to achieve your ultimate goal, seal the deal or get that last percentage point you were holding out for. The Bombshell knows that the smile is one of the most underutilized tools in negotiations and we like to use all of the effective, civilized weapons we possess.

As I am sure we all agree, contacts in business can make or break the foundation on which an individual runs their company. This means that in every possible situation the Bombshell needs to be able to market herself with a smile. So, while the competition is clamoring to make the right contacts at a conference, the Bombshell is enjoying the luxury of colleagues and contacts approaching her. Imagine being able to achieve this simply by being the bright, competent Bombshell that you have discovered you are. Keep in mind that whenever you are in a situation of contact with those you hope to develop a rapport with, you must carry yourself as though these people are watching you at all times because as you are a Bombshell, they likely will be!

"Picture leaving people awash in your glitter...they will be"

"We forget that our sparkle as a Bombshell is an endless resource"

CHAPTER FIVE

Let Your Light Shine

CHAPTER FIVE
Let Your Light Shine

If the eyes are the window to the soul, then I would venture to say that most of us have drawn our emotional blinds! Not you dear Bombshell, but if by some chance you have, it's time to do some ventilating of your soul. Open the windows and let there be an exchange of air and energy that will be the start of something wonderful for you as well as those around you. Eye contact, as we have briefly touched on, is something so powerful and special that few seem to be able to fully develop themselves to effectively utilize this skill. It will become key to conveying everything that you are as a woman and letting others get a feeling for your inner beauty, which is, as we know, essential to becoming a Bombshell!

Remembering that our inner beauty is the key to our sparkle, it seems fitting that we take the most direct route to encourage others to sparkle as well. This may require the removal of a few emotional roadblocks—we want to create an unobstructed view of ourselves for those we choose to share this with. Just when you think that we live in a world of people living apart from each other in every emotional aspect, you will be able to declare an open spirit and show this to others in one well-timed glance. Don't be disheartened if this takes some time to perfect, but keep in mind that once you use eye contact properly, it will become a method of communication unmatched in versatility and results.

Eye Contact for Beginners

This sounds rather basic and you might be tempted to skip over this section, but before you do, take note of your ability to look everyone you meet square in the eyes, if only for a moment. Doing this is likely much more difficult than you ever thought it would be because as a society we have receded to the point where we have shut ourselves off from the human exchange and experiencing each other as people is a thing of the past. When was the last time you noticed the look on the face of your bank teller or neighbor? When you start to analyze your interactions with others, you will be surprised at the way most are removed from the people and objects around them. I'm not telling you too look lovingly into the eyes of the boy loading your groceries into the back of the car (that comes later in the chapter!), but I am most certainly advocating that you look directly at him while you thank him for his help. Developing this habit will ensure your constant acknowledgement of the people you come into contact with. You want every person you meet to feel that you have made an effort to connect with them on a basic human level, showing them the respect that you have for them while allowing them a glimpse of your sparkle makes a surprisingly profound difference in your everyday existence. This may not seem like something of great importance but make no mistake, people can feel when you let them in. They may not be able to articulate why they feel so good after running into you, but communication between two people can be acheived without being overt. It is this feeling of being touched by another person without knowing why and other small accomplishments like this that will ready you for the times of explosive connections that you will be able to experience later on in your Bombshell development. This is easy to do; you just have to let go of old fears and have faith that you are able to give a tiny part of yourself to everyone you choose, and that this is a contagious little gift that can serve no purpose other than to perpetuate overall happiness.

If this seems like an enormous challenge to you, then take things one step at a time and remember that your goal is not to elicit some WWF stare-down competition, just a friendly glance is all it takes to get you started. The steps you take toward this will go miles towards your eventual goal of being able to look anyone in the eye with extraordinary confidence. The small looks that get you started will be enough to prove to you the power of communicating in this fashion. If you know someone who has always made you a little nervous then you have found the perfect test subject for your development. Once you can look that person directly in the eye while interacting with them, you know you have made some serious progress. Remember that you always want to expand your comfort zone and challenge yourself to do things you previously dismissed as "not for you." Everything is possible for you dear Bombshell; it is just a matter of reaching for it.

At first it may seem a little unnatural for you to look so directly at the cashier as he rings up your purchase and it may be hard for you to make a habit of this, but soon you will find that its effectiveness is enough encouragement to keep you on track. A Bombshell will always acknowledge people in the same manner, regardless of their status—unless it is a romantic interest. If you are not quite confident enough to tackle this with complete strangers then try it on people you are close to, like family and friends. I promise you that they won't be able to tell what you are doing differently, but they will definitely notice the change in your demeanor. The key to beginning is knowing that the eye contact, although direct, should only last as long as the conversation or the "Thank you so much"; any longer than that and you risk looking a little too intense!

Once you manage to make the effort of eye contact a habit, you can move on to more challenging situations to test your progress.

Do It Bombshell-style: Activity

Approach a total stranger and engage him in some kind of conversation, maintaining eye contact at all times. Even if you just begin by asking for the time, you will be gaining useful experience for social events or other situations that previously made you feel uncomfortable. It will evolve very quickly into an enjoyable exchange for you and leave you feeling that you have connected with a total stranger, even if only on a very basic level.

These strategies for building self-confidence are really about reprogramming yourself to allow your sparkle a channel out of which it can flow freely and the eyes are certainly one of the most personal and important portals.

The point of making a visual connection with people is that you are able to give them an honest vision of what you want to express about your thoughts and feelings. Even if you are dealing with an issue that is not what you really want to talk about there are ways of getting your point across without having to say anything aloud. For instance, if you are in a situation where you are lost and in desperate need of some direction, you will find that people will make a much greater effort to assist you when you convey your feelings to them with a genuine glance of distress. The same thing goes for asking the clerk for a discount on those shoes you must have! Hey, I didn't say that eye contact was restricted to certain applications, did I? After all, you are a Bombshell!

Eye Contact for Him

When it comes to the opposite sex, eye contact can be a deadly tool—in that really good, fun kind of way. Of course, when flirting we use all of our Bombshell tricks but without the proper eye contact, our other tricks are only minimally effective. I can tell you from experience that the only men who have ever given me butterflies have been the ones who have made direct, lingering eye contact with me. We are talking the kind of eye contact that shows me he isn't afraid of me and that, in fact, he welcomes the challenge I present to him. Hmm . . . this leads me to believe that the same is true for men. One silent, well-timed, unwavering look can be all that it takes to make his manly bits quiver! Well ladies, now all you need to do is make sure you have the proper tools to implement your magic spell. Upon mastering the previous skills outlined in this book, you will be more than well-equipped to channel your nice (or naughty) thoughts to any man you choose. I can assure you that you will be able to sense the effects almost immediately, so be careful who you decide to use this one with.

Remember dear Bombshell, that by now we have mastered that fine art of walking that proverbial line—even in stilettos! Pertaining to eye contact and the man of your interest, it is important to keep in mind a point I made earlier: men still like to feel as though they make women a little bit nervous. This means that your eye contact, depending on the situation, will be critical when walking that fine line between showing your interest and making him feel slightly superior. If you are looking at a man from across the room but are unable to make your way over to him, then you will want to make obvious eye contact and hold it so that even at a distance he cannot misunderstand the fact that you might be interested, and of course this is always accompanied by some level of smile. Men, like all people, need to feel like they are walking into some element of invitational interaction and not being ambushed.

Once you've used your "come hither" look to get him to approach you it will be key to follow through with more eye contact to seal the deal if that is what you decide your ultimate goal to be. Keeping in mind the "good from far but far from good" credo, you may decide not to pursue it past a warm introduction but the true Bombshell is always gracious and goes out of her way not to injure anyone's feelings.

Don't expect the opposite sex to use eye contact in the same way we do. There are reasons that men and women do things differently and this facilitates the ebb and flow of the relationships in which we may be engaged. Using eye contact in an already established relationship is yet another way to deepen and strengthen the connection you may already have. Think back to the times in your courtship where you would look longingly into his eyes. Now, make a conscious effort to do that on a regular basis. Don't let go of those moments of deep, unspoken communication; these moments will help you to remember who you fell in love with in the first place. A well-timed look into your lover's eyes will still give him goose bumps and will help you keep that love fresh while conveying your feelings for him. The best thing about the unspoken is that there is no need for him to respond; it speaks to him with out expectation. The looks you give him will be very powerful, even when you don't think he notices.

Also, dear Bombshell never let go of the lusty looks that made him weak from the start! Any good relationship will sustain itself if you put the same efforts into keeping him as you did to get him because sadly, if you don't, someone else may try.

CHAPTER SIX

Carriage—Not Just Locomotion

CHAPTER SIX
Carriage—Not Just Locomotion

Bombshell, do you know what carriage is? If you do, do you know how to use it? Without a doubt, this is one of the most important elements of being a Bombshell. So powerful it can speak volumes without so much as a whisper, good carriage can convey sexy and confident, it can say "Don't even think about messing with me 'cause it can't be done!" or it can say "I'm capable of loving and being loved" and everything in between. What exactly is so powerful about a form of locomotion that it can convey all of these things and so much more? How do you come to emanate this aura at all times? Let me give you the basic outline of self-presentation that will give you such undeniably fabulous carriage that even the Queen of England will wonder who should bow to whom!

One of the interesting things about carriage is that it is almost a literal term in some ways. It is your flow, your posture and the way that you transport yourself from place to place both physically and in a more ethereal sense. A gorgeous woman can be downgraded to mediocre just by walking poorly. If you think that I am exaggerating, watch a reality matchmaking show and count the number of women who walk like male truckers and those whose sloping shoulders and poor posture indicate low self-esteem. The few women on these shows who have great carriage were walking tall, straight-backed and taking feminine, confident steps. This may be new to some of you, but if you start to look around at the most accomplished women in the world, you will see that their shoulders are not rounded, their heads are lifted and you will certainly never see them walking like they're wearing hip-waders.

Have you ever taken a self-defense class? Did you know that one of the main teachings in self-defense is walking with purpose? This is done specifically so that if you are being sized-up by a potential assailant, he will realize quickly that you are not a woman to consider attacking. In my coaching I teach the same thing, only I modify it to an ultra-feminine and sexy standing that will convey a confidence and warmth with each step. To do this you must remember that your inner feelings of self-confidence must be allowed to flow through you and be visible to those surrounding you. It is imperative for you to realize that everything you believe about yourself will be conveyed in your action. As a Bombshell you will feel spectacular and will leave those you breeze by feeling like spring air.

Learning to Walk Like a Bombshell

The first thing to do if you know that your walk needs a little work is to go and rent some movies—new and old—so that you can watch the women you admire in action. This may seem strange to you but it will be a fun research project for you to do when you know what you are looking for. You could even do this with a few friends, some hors d'oeuvres and a bottle of wine. This isn't supposed to be torture, but remember that it will take some work to override the posture you have been sporting since puberty! Just remember that the unspoken can convey much more than you think, and it can do so instantaneously. There is no other action as powerful in its benign state. Once you decide on a style of walk that you find comfortable and intriguing, make it your own. Remember at all times that the Bombshell is original and that the guidelines I give you are only meant to be the tools with which you can uncover what works best for you while remaining true to yourself and your goal of becoming the best Bombshell you can be. Practice as much as possible, even if this is while you are walking the aisles of the grocery store. You will want to adapt this refined walk for everyday as carriage is not for special occasions, it is forever. If you are finding the walk a challenge to master, call your local modeling school and they can help you fine tune it. Just because you aren't a runway model doesn't mean you can't walk like one when necessary!

The only time I would suggest becoming a little more coquettish in your walk is when you are in social situations where you want to knock someone's socks off. When these times arrive and you find yourself at the same event as the man you've been fantasizing about, it is definitely okay to use a little more hip and walk a little slower to emphasize that you are not afraid to be noticed by him and the entire room. Don't be afraid of this Bombshell, as once your transformation is complete the only disadvantage you can expect is having less time to enjoy your cocktail—people will be stopping you to chat!

This purposeful yet sexy walk is generally accompanied by a gentle, knowing smile because carriage is not just about the walk; it is about every nuance you convey to the world.

In its display of the visual and the all-important intangible, carriage is proof that what you can't see is as important as what stares you in the face. When you hear people speak of that *je ne sais quoi* you will understand what they mean. When you carry yourself like the newly polished Bombshell you are, the things you have discovered about yourself will begin to spill over into other parts of your life. You will start to get better treatment in restaurants, people will respond well to you on the street and maybe your boss will even see that you are the best person for the promotion being considered. Wonderful things will begin to happen as soon as the cosmos realize that you are ready for them. When you walk around and leave people in the wake of your Bombshell glitter you will know that you are finally letting your body language express your most wonderful qualities with every move you make.

Enlist Help!

If you are ever in doubt about your newfound carriage have a few men give you their opinion. Ironically, some men are exceptionally good at determining what works well for a woman. If you are a little too fresh to demonstrate it for them, then fast forward your study movies and show them a few clips of what you have been working on. Don't be discouraged if they don't have the exact same opinions as you on this one because it is what feels best for you that counts. Get them to tell you which women they think have that special something and do your own research on these women, be they starlets, politicians, newscasters, sports figures or family members. You may be surprised by the number of these women who have carriage that is not only about their physical attributes, and I will tell you this: I am a blonde, blue-eyed woman with breast implants and there is nothing new about that. But, when you see me walk by, you will notice that my uniqueness is astoundingly obvious. It won't be anything you can put your finger on; it will be that haze of happy, positive energy that the Bombshell exudes. Carriage will go a very long way in helping you portray this same positivity to the people with whom you are fortunate enough to interact with.

Common Carriage Mistakes and Locomotion

There are a few things to avoid when it comes to your carriage Bombshell, and many of them are simply bad habits formed in childhood, or even just from a lack of body awareness. What I mean by this is that you need to be consciously aware of your movements while feeling your physical presence and be able to make adjustments to your body and mind simultaneously so that you can subtly but effectively convey your confidence.

A Bombshell never lets her posture escape her—we simply don't do it! The rounding of a woman's shoulders or the curving forward of her spine scream that she is insecure and afraid of being noticed. I can't imagine wanting to convey a message as negative as the ones that bad form can send to anyone, let alone people who you are meeting for the first time and who are beginning to form their opinion of you. Don't ever let your body take the form of anything other than tailored, upright and lady-like as this is the form that will carry you through dates and meetings alike. Carriage is least about locomotion, despite it carrying the Bombshell from place to place, and is more about a constant, silent communication being used by you to further connect with others.

Another mistake we Bombshells avoid is allowing our bodies to betray our state of mind. This is a point of note because even the most seasoned Bombshell has moments when she is feeling rattled. This is normal from time to time, but is not to be conveyed by our body language. You've heard of poker face? Well, dear Bombshell, we have the "poker body" as well. Never let a minor fluster keep you from standing tall and walking proudly because it may well be that this posture is the very thing to facilitate your recovery from that brief moment of doubt. If anyone is watching you, which is a given at this point in your journey, you want to show them that your carriage is unwavering and that it will see you through with a poise that is unmatched.

Don't underestimate the power of your carriage and always remember that it carries you many more places than you previously realized. If you remember to make this posture an automatic element of your demeanor then it will be a constant comfort to you and will be always at the ready. I cannot stress enough that to know the power of your carriage is to know the power of the woman behind it and it will see you through many different situations, both easy and enjoyable or challenging and disarming.

This will become your permanent grace on command and will serve you in ways you never knew possible.

Many women mistake strong carriage for an aura of arrogance and this is a Bombshell no-no. The last thing we want is to be perceived as unapproachable or haughty. As a true Bombshell you will want to do everything in your power to have your carriage convey your sense of self in the best way possible as it shows those around you that you are a confident, good person on the whole; this means walking tall, with a smile and relaxed in your stride. Don't make the mistake of feeling better than everyone else. The only thing you want to feel is that you are shining, being the best woman you possibly can. All good Bombshells will rebuke the idea of arrogance as we know that this is just the mask of insecurity—one that we won't wear, Bombshell. Visualize yourself as an open book to those watching you and this will help them to feel comfortable when they are in your presence. Just watch the changes occur when you start walking a little taller, prouder and more confidently.

CHAPTER SEVEN

Finding the Perfect Fit

CHAPTER SEVEN
Finding the Perfect Fit

I t's time to look at the wrapping paper we use to present our gifts to the world. Perhaps that sounds a little ostentatious, but if you think about it, we live in a world where packaging and marketing are everything, so why would we think that Bombshells are in any way exempt from this? I hate to admit it, but pretty bows, wrapping and other trappings can make even the most typical gift really exciting to open. Well dear Bombshell, let's see how we can apply this to ourselves and still have a little fun with it! Remember that by now you have much more of the emotional infrastructure needed to carry all of the beautiful trimmings without caving in under the weight of it all!

The Closet Clean Out

Sounds painful, huh? Well, it can be if you are the sort of person who never throws anything out and buys things just because they are on sale. I hate to say this but we are only hurting ourselves when we buy strictly based on price. Throughout this chapter I will share some wonderful money-saving ideas to help you dress like a Bombshell and still maintain your savings account. It can be done, so make sure you add these to your Beauty File so you can grab them and go at a moment's notice because you never know when you will get wind of a last minute sale!

We have to face certain wardrobe facts, Bombshell. Styles change and this means that your wardrobe should, too. Every couple of years you should expect to endure the pain of getting rid of your favorite pair of jeans. It won't be easy and you need to understand that what you paid for them or who you met when you wore them doesn't matter. The same goes for things like shoes and boots. Eventually you will have to adopt the "out with the old and in with the new" credo. Now I know that this can be expensive (or just plain old fun if you have tons of cash to blow) but I will give you some wonderful tips that you will be able to use anywhere in the world.

Go Fantasy Shopping

This sounds like fun, doesn't it? Well, it can be and it serves a few fantastic and potentially money saving purposes. We Bombshells love to wear designer labels but we would really rather not pay full price for them. Now, when I say fantasy shopping I mean get dressed nicely and hit some very upscale department stores in your area. The point of this little venture is to try on as many different styles and designers as you can to see which ones you love and which ones love you. Keep a Beauty File card with you on this outing as you will want to write down what labels fit you well and what sizes you wear in certain brands. If you feel like your bank account can handle some action, feel free to pick up some choice items, but this is primarily intended to be a research trip. Remember not to be intimidated walking into these high-priced havens, you are as worthy and as beautiful as the next shopper, so walk in like you could buy the whole place if you wanted to but keep it light-hearted!

Once you have made your designer wish list it is time to make room in your closet. This will undoubtedly require the help of friends, perhaps Bombshells themselves. Open yourselves a bottle of wine (not whine) and have that closet cleaning party. You need to make sure that your friends are being ruthless and that you have plenty of garbage bags on hand. Anything out of date, ripped, fading, ill-fitting or just plain wrong will be tossed or donated accordingly. This is not the time for sentimentality ladies! The select items we keep for special reasons should be removed from the closet and relegated to storage or a keepsake box. Don't forget to do the same with your shoes and boots.

I'm sure that by now you will have lots of room in your closet for your new and improved Bombshell wardrobe. So now that you are armed with your Beauty File notes and designer wish lists, I recommend you start cutting out photographs from fashion magazines like *InStyle, Flare, Vogue* or *People* to get good ideas about what's "in" right now. Especially useful are the magazines that show you how to switch up a number of basic pieces to make many more looks than you thought possible. Keep in mind that not every style you like will like you, be realistic in your expectations and be willing to modify styles to suit your body type and Bombshell personality.

Armed with your Beauty File, grab a friend and get started on a day of bargain hunting. Once you know the names of the designers whose garments really flatter you, you will be able to identify the sorts of things that suit your body best before you even read the label. There are many stores that carry designer labels at up to fifty percent off the suggested retail price and as a smart Bombshell, you will look for the opportunity to save. Stores like Winners, Ross' and Marshalls can provide the patient Bombshell with some amazing designer clothes at a fraction of the normal cost. Take your time on these expeditions and don't expect to get all of what you are looking for in one day as this simply won't happen—even if you are willing to pay full retail price!

Copying the Looks You Love

It is very easy to put together the looks that you love when you are armed with a photograph. Having this in hand gives you a quick point of reference, but remember that these are only guidelines to help you along the way. The true Bombshell always makes any look uniquely her own by modifying it to suit her preferences and the occasion. We are always trend-aware but prefer to start the trends instead of following them. That being said, start shopping Bombshell, as your newly-packed social calendar is fast-approaching.

> **Tip:** Most upscale department stores and malls have wardrobe consultants available free of charge and by appointment. At no cost to you, why not make use of this expertise? If the prospect of this makes you a little nervous, then go with a close friend.

Remember that an outfit has to make you feel fabulous, so if you are not one hundred percent comfortable with a certain style, then don't wear it. Bombshells are never slaves to the latest trends; we just bear them in mind and make them our own.

So now that you are becoming familiar with the styles and fashions you love, it is time to put together some essential outfits that will be able to take you anywhere with a few modifications. The first thing you need is a pair of dynamite black pants. More than one is optimum but if you have a choice between one out of-this-world, your-thighs-have-to-have-'em pair and another that are perhaps a little more trendy, go for the good fit.

Don't worry, people will be so taken with your sense of style that they won't notice if you wear them twice in a row. These black pants are essential to any Bombshell's wardrobe and can be dressed up or down depending on your social or business requirements. Remember that poor-fitting clothes are not an option, so if need be, invest a little more to get the best fit. I will show you the ways to look the part without sending yourself to the poorhouse, but this is not the item to save money on.

Now for big item number two: a fant*ass*tic (no, I did not misspell that) pair of jeans. This is essential for the Bombshell because great jeans can go anywhere with you and can do pretty well anything for you, even at a moment's notice. You know what I'm talking about and you'll have to get used to the idea of buying a new pair just about every other year. There is no way around this. You will need to bring a friend when you go shopping for them as it can often be a very daunting task. Don't underestimate the power of a great pair of jeans, be they size two or eighteen. Put these with high heels and a silk top and you are ready for anything! Throw them on with great boots and a little t-shirt and you have instant attitude.

> **Tip:** Once you invest in a good pair of jeans, you can pair them with less expensive tops from some of the shops I mentioned earlier. As long as you anchor your look with quality denim it doesn't matter if your top is an old shirt from your boyfriend's closet!

Also, shop end of season for things that tend to be less dependent on climate changes, like t-shirts and jeans. Even lingerie is affected by seasonal changes, so you can get some great bargains to wear year round at a decent discount!

The Safety Outfit

Alright, I will be expecting a thank you card for this one. Henceforth, every Bombshell shall keep a safety outfit cleaned and ready to go at a moment's notice. Every woman has at least one tried and true ensemble that will go to almost any event, never makes us feel fat and always feels good to put on. Never be without this hanging and ready to go, otherwise you can rest assured that you will get that once in a lifetime invitation and you'll be scrambling for something to throw on. The same goes for that perfect little black dress—clean and ready to go! There is something magical about a woman who feels sexy and comfortable; the rest of the room won't know if you wore that outfit twice already that week. Do keep this outfit current, Bombshell; it will have to be redone on a yearly basis as we don't want to look out of date. Remember, a true Bombshell wears her clothes, they do not wear her.

The Conversation Piece Accessory

Now Bombshell, very soon after starting your journey into the sisterhood you will be ready to get noticed almost everywhere you go and you may even start to crave the fun of it. Every successful Bombshell has a few really cool and unusual accessories, and guess what? She isn't afraid to wear them. These can be hats or belts or jewelry but it absolutely must be something that is different, will withstand the changing trends and causes people to ask you about it. Nothing says Bombshell like a woman wearing something no one else could pull off. Remember, we carry these things off easily, as it is part of an expression of our style and fearlessness that is so Bombshell!

> **Tip:** Take that pair of jeans that shrunk in the dryer and have them cropped to the hottest capri style.

> **Tip:** Look for new and unusual things at craft fairs. I bought a fantastic piece of handmade jewelry by a little known artist for next to nothing and now, not only is he famous, but that piece has gone up in value!

The Discount

Don't be afraid to ask for a discount. If there is a mark on an item of interest to you, ask the manager to see what he or she can do for you, but remember to be reasonable in your request.

And don't forget about the ever-fabulous price adjustment! This can be a big one. Have you ever seen something you bought at full price go on sale a week later? Well, take in your receipt and ask for the store policy on adjustments. You would be shocked to know how many large retailers will automatically give you the difference.

Heads and Toes

When we think of accessories, we often forget about the small but important parts of the Bombshell, like hair play. Nothing is more interesting and exotic than a beautiful, fresh flower in your hair. This is something a little out of the ordinary and can be a real conversation starter when people inquire about the type of flower it is or whether or not it is real. We Bombshells thrive on the unexpected and aren't afraid to use the element of fashion surprise! Don't be afraid to try things that you have seen in magazines or fashion shows; just make sure that you feel confident. Try modifying things to suit your mood or event but whatever you do, don't limit yourself based on trying to blend in with the crowd. Shine.

Shoes. Aaah. I feel your rapture fellow Bombshell! This is one of those fashion topics that I am most passionate about. This is a genuine addiction for many of us and although I have yet to smoke or snort a pair, I too, am highly addicted. I am not only an advocate for those who are shoe dependent but I am also all for getting the most beautiful shoes at the most reasonable price. Every once in a while you may have to bite the bullet and pay full price for that perfect pair, but hey, that is just part of being a woman!

As every good builder will tell you, the key to a beautiful home is the foundation upon which it is built and the view it affords the owner. Well Bombshell, that is exactly what shoes should be for you and your style. You need to understand how dramatically shoes can transform both the outfit and the woman who wears them. There is no way to properly convey the importance of high quality, updated and well-maintained footwear. Shoes can make or break your ensemble as well as your ankles!

If I could tell women only one thing pertaining to shoes it would be to always forgo quantity for quality. Given a choice, I would never buy another pair of mediocre shoes when I could behave myself and save up for a fantastic looking and feeling pair. It is a difficult urge to resist, but once you master it and walk in to buy the shoes you thought were out of reach you will realize it was worth the wait. A little tip I used to get past the "but they were black and on sale!" urge: every time I felt I was about to slip, I would go and buy bubble gum. Really, I would not buy plain old mint or cinnamon chewing gum, but back to my childhood, great-big-bubble-blowing, fruity-flavored gum. Then, I would continue walking through the mall blowing silent bubbles inside my mouth. Crazy, but it worked.

I stopped buying those $85 "bargain" pairs and in no time I was buying $300 pairs that I loved so much I would sleep with!

The Fashion File will be an important tool to use when buying shoes. Use it like you do your Beauty file and keep pictures of shoes that you absolutely love and start a little hunt for them. This can be fun and if you can afford the exact ones in the magazines, then go for it, and if not, either start saving or look for a similar pair at a lower price point. One thing is carved in stone Bombshell: do not buy cheap shoes! They will look cheap, they will feel cheap and they can take you down a fashion notch even if you are wearing an expensive outfit. Bear in mind that you will be walking and standing in these; they are quite literally the foundation of what you are wearing.

It is so much better to own a few pairs of fantastic shoes than forty pairs of junkie or outdated ones. If you need to confirm this, start adding up what you paid for them and look in the latest fashion magazine you have to see how you could have invested that money more wisely. Scary, huh? I promise you that when you put on your first pair of designer shoes you will realize very quickly why they cost the hundreds of dollars marked on the price tag. You will walk taller and in much more comfort. It will amaze you to experience walking in a four-inch heel pain-free when previously it killed you to even stand in a pair of two-inchers! The quality is unmistakable and when you know that you are wearing something spectacular, your confidence level will increase (and so will your height). Even when you are just wearing jeans and a t-shirt you know that the foundation of your look is a stunning, sexy pair of shoes that are just waiting to be admired—much like the Bombshell herself. Having the confidence of a Bombshell on the inside will allow you to wear things on the outside that would once have intimidated you, so enjoy!

Don't be afraid of color when choosing your shoes. Yes, we all need a solid pair of basic black pumps, but we certainly don't need ten. Keeping in mind that I have always viewed the word "need" as an expletive, there are few of us who have an unlimited shoe budget. So, the following is what I would recommend as a minimum for every Bombshell:

- One pair of closed-toe, black leather pumps;
- One pair of strappy, high, black sandals; and,
- Two pairs of fabulous fall boots (one in a neutral tone and one in black).

Now for the fun essentials that are necessary all the same:

- One pair of gold or silver sandals;
- One pair of nude colored shoes, open or closed-toe as long as they aren't too chunky; and,
- One pair of wish shoes that you will hopefully get one day.

These highly coveted shoes will be the ones you throw on to add that extra little sprinkle of femininity.

Walk a Mile in Those Shoes

We have already gone over choosing those beautiful, sexy high heels, but lest we forget, we must know how to walk in them. It doesn't matter how expensive your shoes were or how exclusive the designer is if you don't know how to wear them it is all for not. A lady will always wear her shoes, never allowing her shoes to wear her. What I mean is that you will walk with such grace and poise in these shoes that you won't be a teetering, toppling mess of Italian leather prancing around a social function or work event hoping no one notices how precariously perched you are. Practice makes perfect and shoes are by no means an exception to this rule. The better quality your shoes are, the easier you will find them to walk, dance or catch a cab in. Any new shoes should be worn around for at least a day or two before going out in them unless you are a seasoned veteran of the war on bunions! Wear them around the house and outside to scuff up the soles sufficiently to give yourself some grip. The more confident you become, the more you will shine without distraction and this is more important than any Manolo Blahniks (though some might try to argue that one. . .).

> **Tip:** Ask for gift certificates for special occasion instead of those coffee mugs etc. Combine them together and all of a sudden the shoes you thought you could never have suddenly come closer to your reach. Even a few $20 gift certificates can make a big difference on the whole!

> **Tip:** Don't be afraid to play with temporary decorations for your staple black sandals, sometimes replacing the ankle strap with a wide satin ribbon can make your shoes into something spectacular while maintaining their original versatility.

Tip: Try wearing two of the same shoe in different colors. Sounds crazy but when black and white is all the rage, why be afraid to take it all the way down to your shoes?

Speaking of toes, don't forget our earlier teachings of our foot maintenance: hairy toes and open-toed shoes are just wrong, wrong, wrong! There is no point displaying beer nuts in the finest crystal bowl, so remember that when your feet are in a beautiful pair of shoes, they are also being displayed. There is nothing worse than horrible feet being proudly bared in beautiful shoes, so remember to stay on top of your pedicure, whether you get it done at the spa or do it at home. I mean really, if you had a blemish on your forehead, would you circle it in gold and place a jewel above it? I hope not! If you have problem feet that simply cannot be fixed by way of a proper pedicure, then opt for glamorous closed-toe shoes that have a unique heel or unusual design. We Bombshells like to draw attention to our best features, not our worst.

Handbags and Holders

Every woman knows the importance of a good bag, but that doesn't mean that every woman can afford a good designer handbag. Fortunately, there are a few things you can do to remedy this dilemma. The best advice I can give you is to keep it simple when it comes to your collection unless you can afford every color and style. But for Bombshells on a budget, the most important thing is to cover the basics. One great black day bag, one in brown and one in white or a lighter, summery color and at least one good evening clutch are essential. These should cover all your bases and any additional bags would be a nice luxury.

There are a few ways to choose your bags, but I suggest always staying with the classics. A good bag that will stand the test of time is the classic brown monogrammed Louis Vuitton bag. Now this is a bag you will be able to pass on to your daughters and will still be in style, even as a desirable vintage piece. The problem with bags like the wonderful Louis is that they tend to be rather expensive. The best way to cut costs on a fantasy purse like this is to go on eBay and take a look around. You are pretty well guaranteed to find a classic bag at a cost far removed from the original price. The good thing about eBay is that it is a reputable operation. Be sure to get proof of authenticity before making the purchase or you will be mighty disappointed when you discover that you paid a decent sum for a knock off. Don't necessarily go for the latest print in a bag like this as they are often passing trends and will never last as long as the classic ones.

Of course the Bombshell bargain hunter likes to find the best deals she can, so whenever possible, it is a good idea to pop into the outlet malls. Even some of the higher-end stores, like Saks Fifth Avenue, have locations in these malls and you can often find some high quality merchandise that you love there but at a deeply discounted price. These are the best places to look for a simple, black, every day designer bag. These are also the places to find great designer evening bags, but if you rarely use these bags I recommend going to a little bridal shop or other discount-type store and picking up a little beaded bag that can be worn with most of your evening apparel. No designer evening bags are marked on the outside, so let people wonder who designed yours and keep the secret for yourself.

Least Favorite Features

Ask every woman on the planet to name a few body parts she would rather not accentuate and I promise you that even Cindy Crawford would be able to rattle off a list without drawing an extra breath. As I have said before dear Bombshell, physical perfection is not our goal, but wardrobe is a key factor in detracting from our least favorite parts and accentuating the ones we love. When choosing your clothing it is important to remember that some of the most cutting edge styles don't work for everyone. Perhaps this is due to age or body type, or maybe not, but it all depends on the areas you want to draw attention to. Just because it looks good on Britney Spears or Nicole Kidman doesn't mean it will work for you. And in Britney's case Mr. Blackwell seems to think that her clothing selection leaves much to be desired anyway!

Back to our amazing features! Make a list of your most loved body parts. Choose the things you know are exceptional and make an effort to expand your wardrobe based on this list.

If micro-mini skirts are in fashion and you have fantastic legs, then by all means, go ahead and indulge, but if that isn't an area you feel comfortable with then you should know that not even the most expensive designer skirt is going to make you feel good. Every year there will be different styles and there will be trendy pieces for top and bottom, so if you have beautiful arms, then focus the attention on your upper body and keep all eyes where you want them—on you and your favorite bits. If you are still in the process of getting into healthy shape and you can't decide what you like or dislike about your body, then stick with monochromatic colors and some funky jewelry to enhance your face and the positive energy you are putting forth. Be fearless in your focus on positivity: it is your best friend and you have earned the right to feel absolutely radiant by virtue of the efforts you have already made.

Don't Try Too Hard

Sometimes, even for Bombshells, less really is more. I will elaborate because I want don't want there to be any "Less? Like bursting out of my shirt à la Anna Nicole Smith?" going on. This is always wrong (in public anyway!). What I am referring to are the times when everyone else looks like they have spent four hours getting their hair up in ringlets and the Bombshell arrives looking fresh, slightly tousled and immediately sets herself apart from the others (and I don't mean socially). It is wonderful for the Bombshell to walk in and see what look to be almost painful efforts on the part of some women. While I certainly want to spend time on myself before I go out, I want it to look like I enjoyed that time, not like I slaved over my hair and make-up for hours.

With the advent of a more laid-back style being adopted around the world, it can be great fun for the Bombshell to rely on her internal glitter sometimes. We can make anything look beautiful and glamorous, so why not have a little fun with an outfit that you know is just below the fashion radar but because it is on you, it outshines even the most lavishly beaded gown.

I always recommend making the effort to dress beautifully wherever and whenever, but choose the focus of your outfit. The one big mistake many women make is having way too much going on, or over-accessorizing. What I mean is, if you have a stunning and sparkling pair of shoes, you will want your bag to be simple and classic.

If you are wearing a micro-mini, don't pair it with a plunging neckline. The same is true of the fabulous accessories you wear. Don't pair huge chandelier earrings with a large necklace; they will only fight for attention visually and end up detracting from the true sparkle, which is you.

"Carriage is not just propelling yourself; it is projecting yourself"

"Property value goes way up with a little landscaping"

CHAPTER EIGHT

Restoration Work, Anyone?

CHAPTER EIGHT
Restoration Work, Anyone?

Y ou didn't really think a book like this would totally ignore the option of cosmetic surgery now did you? Listen Bombshell, I will give you my opinion on the subject but ultimately you will have to decide how you feel about permanently altering or enhancing your physical being for yourself. Just remember that the biggest changes will happen inside of you and that confidence always ages gracefully.

I find that the latest fads in cosmetic surgery are the smaller, less invasive procedures like the lunch hour facelift. It is really quite funny: you go in for an hour and ask for the female equivalent of the extra value meal—a mini facelift with some injectable filler and some Botox on the side! Procedures these days read like a fast food menu without the calories and the fat injected only where you want it. This is kind of cool for the Bombshell who chooses to go this route and select from the surgeon's menu but it is not necessary to achieve true beauty!

> **Tip:** Many surgeons do different kinds of demonstrations throughout the year, so once you get to know and trust a doctor, you can volunteer to be the next one in front of a group giving you a possible freebie!

I will tell you from my own experiences that surgeries like these can be both good and bad, but the most important thing to remember is that cosmetic surgery will never make you beautiful, but it can help keep your appearance that way for a little longer. Bear in mind that a Bombshell's love of who she is on every level is what makes her so attractive. There may be times in your life when you have the opportunity to correct something that you always thought looked a little out of place and that the little (or not so little) things that may bother you are often not too difficult to remedy, so don't feel any unearned guilt about doing what it takes to make yourself feel that extra bit more confident.

Now is probably a good time to tell you my personal experience with the ever-popular boob job. I was twenty-something and had already given birth to two beautiful girls, one aged five and the other nine months. I really believed that after pushing fifteen pounds out of my precious parts and seventy-two total laboring hours that I should have been rewarded by the gods and restored to my former self. Ha! Clearly the joke (rather cruelly) was on me. Even though I was back to my original weight and my stomach was flat, so were my once perky breasts. I suppose having them filled with life-giving fluid for eighteen months had taken its toll on my boys. They weren't getting up; I could stand on my head and use them for eye patches but there was no way they were ever going to re-inflate themselves to their former glory. So I found myself with the body of a twenty-something and the breasts of my great-grandmother. This did not befit the Bombshell I knew myself to be, so I decided to do something about it.

After much research, education and thought, I had what I now call my "restoration work." I found a wonderful surgeon, took my time to heal and was incredibly happy with the results. Yes it hurt and yes they look spectacular, but more importantly, I feel like I got my breasts back—and well deservedly. The only thing I can say to you is that this type of surgery is incredibly personal and should be used only as a way to make yourself feel better without it becoming the foundation of yourself. Any woman who thinks that a cosmetic procedure will "make" her a Bombshell is sorely mistaken and will be badly let down. I was a Bombshell long before my breast surgery and will remain one forever because of the work I have done on myself as a woman from the soul out. I am always amused when people think that they can buy self-esteem in a little silicone cup. It doesn't work that way, so don't be fooled!

The good news on the cosmetic front is the evolution of smaller, more preventative steps that we can take to stave off the inevitabilities of time and its mambo across our faces. The list is endless—there are so many options to take into consideration but none of them should be undergone without serious thought and an honest look at your motivations. Of course there are some things that you can do that have a more temporary effect than actual surgery and can give you an idea of what to expect from a more permanent change, but all of these things range from "costly" to "very expensive," so be thoughtful in your decision making. A surgeon is not someone who should be chosen based on cost. I am a huge believer in saving money, but this is one area where corners cannot afford to be cut!

Choosing Your Doctor

Looking for a surgeon should be a little bit like looking for a friend. It is most important to ensure that the qualifications of your new medical expert are current and legitimate, but I think that goes without saying. Consultations are your best way of testing the waters with a potential candidate and although they can be costly, most doctors will deduct it from the cost of your procedure if you choose to go with them. I cannot stress strongly enough the importance of a good rapport between you and your doctor. You cannot have any reservations about communicating with this person and if you feel you aren't being heard or that your concerns are not being addressed, then you need to interview more physicians. I have met a few doctors who were condescending toward me and I took this as a clear message that this person was too self-engrossed to properly manage my health and well-being.

Celeste speaks:

I never thought I would venture into the world of cosmetic surgery, but the aging of my inner and outer selves had been off-pace and I wanted to see if I could somehow match the two. Although I know that I will remain youthful on the inside for years to come and that my body will continue to age despite my protestations, I decided that I would try to curb the changes of my aging body by indulging in smaller, less invasive procedures like Botox and some line-erasing to try and slow the signs of time. I have found a wonderful doctor who understands my needs and treats me accordingly. Now I feel like my two selves are closer to being a match than before and my friends and family say that this comes through in my disposition!

I can't say that this Bombshell has anything against buying a sexy new pair of lips or avoiding crow's feet where possible, but remember that everything is good in moderation dear Bombshell, as we want to make an impression based on who we are and not on what we purchase! On that note, I am also a big fan of being honest with others about any work that one may choose to have done. I do this for several reasons: firstly, a true Bombshell knows that to stand on the truth is to stand on an unshakeable foundation, and secondly, what if other women who have had children think it's normal for breasts to look like mine after breastfeeding two children? That would be so wrong! It is a very personal choice to divulge any cosmetic work you may have had done; who wants to admit they had a little help? Well Bombshell, look at it this way, most things in life require some sort of help. I mean, my breasts wouldn't have looked that way in the first place without the help of my two little babies and I was just tipping the scales back into my own favor.

"When the successful Bombshell enters any room people will stop and notice, not because she is clapping and laughing and jumping up and down but because her soul is clapping and laughing and jumping up and down"

CHAPTER NINE

Making an Entrance and
Leaving an Impression

CHAPTER NINE
Making an Entrance and Leaving an Impression

N ow that we have addressed most of the Bombshell's physical and aesthetic requirements, I can start to show you what to do with all of your newfound sparkle. By now you are really starting to feel like the woman you always wanted to be and it's time to start showing it to others. The first thing you need to keep in mind is that you are most beautiful when you feel that way inside. It may seem strange, but everything that runs through your mind will often be translated through your body and the way you carry yourself. In this chapter I will talk about how to make an unforgettable entrance, regardless of the place, time or event.

From charity balls to business meetings, there is one very powerful asset that the Bombshell should utilize at all times: the ability to make a legendary first impression. Good or bad, this first encounter can be a challenge, so let's make yours spectacular. There are so many ways to make a magical entrance, though one must keep in mind the nature of the event as it is not in the Bombshell's best interest to behave inappropriately.

The Business Affair

All good businesswomen know how difficult it can be to command the respect and attention of her peers. As your inner Bombshell develops, this ability to lead will become second nature. At most business social affairs, your co-workers will be a little worn from the work day and their exterior presentation may reflect their inner exhaustion. A true Bombshell does not subscribe to this image as we pride ourselves on a portrayal of fresh and readiness. This prepared and alert reflection is one that is undeniably important when there is valuable time with your boss at stake! Hopefully you will know about any significant events or meetings well ahead of time so that you can bring at least a partial change of clothes with you. Unless this is an office cocktail party, an entire change in wardrobe is not necessary, but going from pants to a skirt or a change in blouse can make a world of difference in the way you feel about yourself going into one of these socials and can allow you to maintain the sense of beauty and accomplishment that your day began with.

If the office event you will be attending is a board meeting or other business-oriented affair, punctuality is a must, so plan to arrive a few minutes early, or at very least, on time. On the other hand, if this is a more social function, then you may certainly feel free to take advantage of the Bombshell's right to be fashionably late! This entrance is the moment that you walk in—preferably alone—and radiate a fresh, confident and friendly energy. This means walking fairly briskly around the entire room with purpose: back straight, head high and minimal, though not with non-existent, coquettish overtones. Keep feeling fantastic about who you are and what you do within your company. Continually remind yourself to exude all of the positive qualities you possess because the aura you give off will draw everyone, including your superiors, to you. People around you will wonder what "it" is that you have that makes such an impression and they will be begging for your recipe for magnetism.

Working the room during various social events is a whole different subject, so we will continue to discuss different daily and social entrances so that you are prepared for any and all events and non-events and leave working the room until later. If you are ever in doubt as to proper dress for one of these events, pull out one of your safety outfits. Regardless of the dress etiquette, always wear what makes you look and feel fantastic because that is of utmost importance and do not be afraid to walk the line and try something new, as long as you remain on the side of good taste.

Kelly speaks:

I knew I was walking, talking and dressing differently, but soon, Mario knew it also! He used to fly through my division to check out the latest blonde administrative assistant until one fateful afternoon. When I saw him coming, I jumped up and floated passed him with Jacqueline's words ringing in my ears: "Leave a wake of your energy behind you." Well, I did, and he stopped dead in his tracks watching me pass. I smiled inside and out. There he was, completely awash in my aura, trying to figure out why he had never noticed me before. Maybe it was because I was finally noticing me!

Social Events Without Complications

The purely social event entrance is by far the most fun for the fully developed Bombshell despite the challenge it may present to the Bombshell-in-Training. Now, when I use the term "social event without complications," I mean that no extenuating circumstances would exist to apply undue pressure to the Bombshell herself. You know what I mean: parties with ex-boyfriends, ex-in laws or other individuals whose company is not positive for the Bombshell. Complications like this can have a radical effect on the nature of your entrance and I will address ways to adapt to situations like this later on in the chapter.

Tip: Borrow an accessory that you adore from a friend. This way, you can feel the excitement of something new without spending any money!

The most important thing to remember in a strictly social entrance is that it is essential to feel glamorous and special; you may not actually be the most beautiful person in the room, but those who are watching you will believe that you are. Perhaps you don't believe me, but I and the women whose stories you are hearing are living proof that all things and levels of progress are possible. To ensure that you make the most stellar entrance possible, make sure that your preparation time is not rushed or stressful. A relaxed and timely dressing will allow for the mental preparation required to solidify the manner in which you will enter any situation. Do whatever is necessary to make yourself feel even more special than you already know yourself to be; have your hair blown dry by your stylist, purchase a new and exciting accessory or something that makes you feel a little bit more confident. However you choose to sparkle, be happy with the way you look and feel because these are the wings that will carry you through another magical evening.

Okay, so now you have arrived at the event and are about to enter. This is the time for the final and most important accessory: your smile! I cannot adequately emphasize the importance of giving off an air of happiness and warmth as this is the single most attractive quality you will ever possess. An openness of spirit and a genuine smile are more valuable assets than any other—they will make any designer gown pale in comparison and can make diamonds seem lack-luster. Now, the Bombshell clearly possesses all of these qualities and the combination of them is simply unparalleled. Always remember that a true Bombshell can glitter in a garbage bag if necessary, but of course, we prefer silk!

Once you walk through that door, it's time to shine. As you walk slowly and gracefully into the room, you will notice that your confidence will be magnetic—people will unable to take their eyes from you. Everyone, and I mean everyone—waiters and waitresses, men and women, adults and children alike—will be drawn to the energy you emanate. A Bombshell never stays in one place too long because she knows that that which is slightly elusive is generally that which is most desirable. I recommend stopping to speak to anyone with whom you are acquainted and implementing the skills you will soon have. A Bombshell always carries herself like a lady, with class and a style that is uniquely her own. That being said, a lady with an escort must always remain respectful and sensitive to the needs of her date, regardless of her feelings towards anyone else at the event.

The key to the "entrance" is to make everyone at the event see how beautiful you are inside before they even think to notice the effort your have put into your exterior.

Social Events With Complications

Now dear Bombshell, you can be sure that a little rain has fallen in every beautiful garden and we can understand this to be true in the lives of all socially active creatures. Occasionally we may find ourselves in anxious or undesirable social situations that can be easily navigated with a little extra finesse. These social situations—like running into an ex and his new love interest at a party, or the knowledge that you will be attending a function with some individuals whose company you would otherwise choose not to keep— are not necessarily easy to get through, but I will do my best to help you avoid social nausea and enjoy yourself. The ability to turn an otherwise unfortunate situation into one in which you can amuse yourself is the gift of the Bombshell because our ample brains and limitless charisma allow for us to exhibit grace under pressure.

Anyone facing the anticipation of attending a function with complications has, perhaps, a little more preparation to do before the big event. If this is your first event with such a level of discomfort, you may be more nervous than usual. These situations can make the Bombshell's grand entrance slightly more complicated, but certainly no less fun! As you deal with the wrenches thrown into your works, remember how incredibly special and wonderful you are and you will successfully project an energy that will automatically deflect any negativity that may cross your path. The notion of needing emotional protection from the world goes right out the window for the Bombshell who knows that most of the negative beings out there will feel you radiate goodness and that will be your automatic force field!

Preparation will be the key to feeling your absolute best. Be sure to give yourself time to relax and mentally prepare for the event—go for a good workout or an afternoon at the spa to perk you up and help you to mentally prepare to give you that extra edge. If you are feeling a little trepidation, try to remember the times when you were able to use your Bombshellhood to captivate a room or event. Positive thinking is a Bombshell's best friend!

Tip: A gown rental service can provide you with the look you want for a formal event without having a serious impact on your bank account.

The Bombshell can nearly always stand on her own but there are times when less than desirable social situations can call for an escort. Please don't ever think that the requirement for this task is a man because this role can indeed be filled by your mother or your best friend, or frankly, anyone else. As long as your date is an individual who is supportive and who carries his or her self with class, you will have a fabulous time. If no one is able to attend the event with you, then just take a deep breath and go it alone—you know you can!

Just before you make your entrance into this slightly more difficult social situation must remember one thing: any scenario you have in your head will be much worse than it could ever really be. As with every other entrance, you will walk tall and with just a little more purpose than usual—like you know exactly where you are headed, even if you have never entered this room in your life. Your smile will portray nothing of your nervousness and as you radiate your Bombshell confidence you will realize that YOU OWN THAT ROOM. Even if you walk right into the individual you may have been hoping to avoid, your gracious smile and "hello" as you pass them will demonstrate the grace and style with which the Bombshell is fully equipped. You have sent the message you desired and whether or not you are civil in nature is of no consequence.

The key to any event or situation that makes you uncomfortable is to use the things that are the most powerful to the Bombshell: smile, laughter and your Signature Move. These are the weapons of a consummate Bombshell and they are so much more effective than dirty looks and snide remarks. Anything or anyone making things difficult for you will be immediately diffused when you enjoy yourself despite the presence of someone whose company you would not choose to keep. To eliminate the tension brought on by these situations, the Bombshell merely has to rely on her own ability to charm the rest of the room and leave those less desirable to fend for themselves. Once people realize that you have an unshakeable confidence and a shine that cannot be muted, they will likely give up on their attempts to thwart the Bombshell and move on—sometimes to the bar for a few too many as he or she prepares to self medicate and wallow in self pity.

Do It Bombshell-style: Activity

Picture your entrance as your walk down a red carpet. I want you to visualize all eyes on you and maintain the stature of your confidence that you have uncovered. As a Bombshell you must understand that opportunities for greatness can present themselves at the most unexpected times and; therefore you will always want to convey your readiness to embrace the special gifts and prospects that you so richly deserve. You never know who is watching you dear Bombshell— you may find yourself in a position to connect with a business or romantic contact that you have always wanted and you may not even realize the good fortune you are in the midst of. Stop wishing Bombshell, and start watching. Make every step one that you can see yourself taking toward your ultimate goals.

Barbara speaks:

I knew it was a possibility; running into my ex was certainly not something I looked forward to, but it was definitely something I was prepared for . . . à la Bombshell! It was a charity event that I had not previously attended, but was very excited about and thanks to my

Bombshell training I was relaxed, looking and feeling fantastic. Just after my first cocktail, I was working the room and ran directly into the cheating, lying scoundrel who I had broken up with just three weeks earlier. A few people at the event who knew our history were expecting drama, but that was not what they got. I walked right up to him, smiling radiantly, and kissed him on the cheek—his date was the one looking a little traumatized! Then, to avoid any further discomfort I introduced myself to her, shook her had warmly then left them there with their jaws dropped while I got myself another glass of champagne, secretly toasting myself!

The Restaurant Entrance

The restaurant entrance can be a great deal of fun, especially after your inner Bombshell has seeped through to the outside. Whether you are meeting friends or a date, the essentials remain the same. Never forget to apply what you have learned as much of the time as possible so that you will be prepared for anything, including the most unexpected.

Regardless of the exclusivity or casualness of the establishment, once you enter the restaurant, make sure you smile and extend your hand to the first person to greet you. Bombshells are always polite and welcoming unless otherwise noted! Try to keep in mind that the maître'd or hostess will be the person who decides where you will be seated for your evening, so a little extra effort toward he or she may go further than you think. Warmth is the key to your success and be sure to make no exceptions—every wait staff, host, chef and bus boy deserves the same degree of respect and attention. Imagine how good your date will feel to enter such an establishment with a woman of such class and integrity! No date? Well then, imagine how this kind of genuine warmth will attract a partner, should that be on your agenda!

Do It Bombshell-style: Activity

Ask your server to introduce you to the owner or chef of the restaurant. In addition to being able to express your appreciation for the wonderful dining experience you have just had, you will also become a "friend" of the restaurant and as a result, a social insider. You will soon see how uplifting it is to show appreciation so intentionally, going to this kind of effort for others is a winning situation for all!

Once you are shown to your table, you should shake the hand of whomever it is that seats you as you thank them. While doing this, maintain eye contact and certainly pass along a smile. Once you sit down, feel free to take in your surroundings, but remember that if you are with a date, behave yourself!

Asking to meet the owner of the establishment or, if he is unavailable, the manager on duty, is a nice extension of appreciation and gratitude. When he or she arrives, be sure to introduce yourself with enthusiasm and rave about the environment of the restaurant. Okay, this may not be applicable to the local greasy spoon, but you should still say hello to the owner of wherever it is that you are dining. Gestures like these will make your inner Bombshell's return to this restaurant easy and glamorous because, you see, everyone likes to feel important and the true Bombshell knows how to make people feel very special.

As any good Bombshell will know, the people you are in contact with are all important, but it is your waiter or waitress who is the person that extra effort should be extended to. Not only does this person deserve courtesy because he or she will be the liaison between you and your meal, but also because they have such an intense and, at times stressful, job. Bombshells make it a priority to try and make people's lives a little happier. There is nothing nicer than being able to refer to your server by his or her proper name and your server being able to use your name when addressing you. Not only is this incredibly respectful, but it also removes any pretension or presumed power structure. As you introduce your Bombshell self to your server, be sure to convey to your server the kind of patron you intend to be: the Bombshell patron!

Do It Bombshell-style: Activity

Introduce yourself to your server and try to use their name when you address them. There is nothing less attractive or polite than addressing your server as "Waiter."

There is absolutely nothing more heinous than a person who thinks it is acceptable to treat wait staff in a dismissive or disrespectful manner. When the Bombshell conveys her warmth to people, it is unconditional—without social boundaries—thus, the Bombshell perpetuates the notion of automatic acceptance of others as well as herself. If you ever have the misfortune to dine with someone who treats staff poorly or who sees the patron as more important than the server: RUN! Run—even in your best shoes—because anyone who engages in this kind of behavior clearly has some issues that extend beyond any of those that the Bombshell may be prepared to embrace.

Minor Culinary Issues

Now, dear Bombshell, onto every silver charger plate a little sauce must spill. The key to any minor dining issues is to handle them with all the grace and charm that the Bombshell possesses. For instance, if you find something wrong with your meal—it wasn't cooked the way you asked or there is something in it that you asked to be removed—very quietly and almost apologetically ask your server to come over. When you are discussing whatever it is that is distasteful to you, perhaps try to take the blame for maybe not having been clear or specific enough. Let your server know what it is that you are finding to be unpalatable and ask if there might be something that can be done. In this instance, it is key that you have already conveyed to the staff that you are a friendly and easy-going patron and that you generally are not the type to be gratuitously difficult. I can promise you that the relationship you establish with your server will go a long way to ensuring that your food arrives back promptly and without any unwanted "additions" from some irate kitchen staff.

After a few return visits to the same great restaurants, you may have afforded yourself little luxuries like being asked to go and say hello to the kitchen staff or perhaps the chef will come out to say hello to you when he hears you are in the house. How wonderful it is for the Bombshell to feel so special and to have made others feel so good about their jobs that they will make the effort to acknowledge your presence. There are a few restaurants that I frequent so regularly that I will actually carry my own plate back to the chef and coyly ask why my meal does not taste the same as the last time I had it. Some chefs will even whip up dishes that are not part of the menu so that I may try something new and spectacular that is being considered for addition to the menu. The important thing here is to have a relationship of mutual respect and enjoyment here because it will go so far towards both you and those around you feeling special. If you can make your arrival an event that is looked forward to, people will remember the fun and pleasure that travels with every Bombshell!

The Bombshell Exit

The art of the Bombshell exit is as important as the entrance: it is memorable and warm. Firstly, I do not condone closing down a restaurant. It is important to leave 'em wanting more. You will graciously thank your sever and the bussing staff, then, ask if you might be able to thank the chef for a wonderful meal—but only if he or she is not swamped. These gestures will tell the restaurant staff that you are willing to make extra efforts to convey your appreciation for their talents. If you are dining with girlfriends, I would suggest that you make it a priority to tip generously (generally, I would say that twenty percent might be a good number); after all, this is how people in the food and beverage business earn most of their income. If by some terrible chance you are on a date and see him horribly under-tipping your wonderful server, take it upon yourself to quietly augment the gratuity by way of a well-timed, cash handshake! Now dear Bombshell, it may begin to happen that the owners of establishments will graciously pick up your dinner tab. If this is the case, be sure to tip your waiter the cash equivalent to what he or she would normally have made.

A Special Case: Sporting Events and The Entrance

Sporting events may not be a Bombshell's biggest strength, but they are still fun, enjoyable and entertaining forums for you to demonstrate just how fabulous—and versatile—the Bombshell truly is. This type of event can be tricky; we do not want to enter painted head to toe in our team colors, but we do want to make an individual statement of support. Blending into the crowd is an option only for those who are afraid to give themselves permission to shine—this is not a part of the Bombshell philosophy; as Bombshells, we want to be noticed in a positive light.

Ushers at sporting events can be likened to the maître'd at a restaurant: they are generally the first person to greet you and they do have the power to move your seats up to ones that may be better than the ones you have tickets for, so as with everyone you encounter, be extra nice!

> **Tip:** Wear something a little out of the ordinary without making a complete spectacle of yourself. For example, dress in your team's colors, in a piece of team nostalgia or, top your outfit off with spectacular hat.

As you enter the arena or stadium, walk slowly down the steps sporting an enthusiastic smile, but watch where you are going so that you don't take a Bombshell tumble down the stairs! (A Bombshell can laugh this off, but we do try to avoid injury at all costs!)

I, as a Bombshell, never take my seat at the same time as the hoards of other people that surround me. To create my own entrance and to afford myself the opportunity to shine without obstruction, I try to wait until things are just about to start so that nothing is missed, but so that there is still my own little runway available!

When you're about to take your seat remember to smile. There is nothing more stunning than a happy, friendly face in a venue where competition is the motivation.

Cheer!

Just because Bombshells are relatively civilized women does not mean that there is any reduction in our enthusiasm for the event we are attending. A sporting event is merely another excuse for the Bombshell to show a little excitement for our team! We are not into the same kind of swearing, screaming, over-the-top kind of ruckus that our male counterparts are, but we are certainly involved in a hearty clap and the odd well-timed cheer. If you have been taken to the event as a guest and do not have much interest in either team, pick the one with the cutest players and root your heart out! By simply choosing a side, you will automatically get into the game and your Bombshell style and zeal will be both infectious and wildly attractive.

Jane speaks:

I was never the bouncy cheerleader type. I always found it easier to give a polite clap for fear that someone might notice me. My Bombshell training certainly changed that for me! I was invited to a major play-off hockey game and was excited yet a little scared. Those games can get pretty rowdy, so I had to find my "game face." The first thing I did was choose an outfit that supported my favorite team; I didn't paint my face or drape myself in a jersey but I was wearing the team colors and a cool team hat. I was so inspired by the reactions I got while finding my seat: people were hooting and waving at me and I was beaming and waving back. The energy from the team support and excitement of others made it so easy to remember my Bombshell sportsman-like conduct. At an event like this, where I would normally have disappeared into the sea of fans, I shone. I cheered with enthusiasm and everyone who looked my way received the biggest, most energetic smile they had ever seen. My team won and so did I!

Regardless of the situation, you need to have fun and trust that you are reaching your fullest potential. Do not allow anyone to rob you of the confidence you have gained and will continue to over the course of your transformation. You have earned all the self-assurance in the world and it is yours alone to keep and enjoy. Give yourself permission to be noticed like every woman deserves to be. If everyone looks at you when you enter a room, then you will know that they are looking to admire you as the Bombshell you are both on the inside and out. Let those around you stare in wonder because your transition is not something to hide, in fact, it is a gift to share with those who you will meet and everyday people everywhere.

Events of any kind have the potential to become exactly what you shape them to be. I remember attending an outdoor charity food-tasting event once. Sounds like fun, right? Well, it was shaping up to be a really wonderful party and I was dressed to the hilt with my favorite new shoes and ever-present optimistic attitude when it started to pour rain! I mean heavens-opening, mud-running, shoe-ruining rain. My girlfriend suggested we go home, but this Bombshell was having none of that! We stayed to enjoy the event in our bare, well-pedicured feet and had an absolute ball.

I wish I had counted the number of women who were watching the fun we were having and decided to do the same. It was a great opportunity to show people how to use what you are given and still be able to enjoy yourself. I like to credit myself with saving many beautiful pairs of shoes as well as our own great time. Every event is what you make it and sometimes that means doing things the unconventional Bombshell way!

CHAPTER TEN

That Thing You Do—The Signature Move

CHAPTER TEN
That Thing You Do—The Signature Move

Just so you know, this section of my book is one of the most personal and was certainly the most difficult to write. Some of the things you will read in this chapter are like top secret recipes that you'll never want to pass along. The things I'll divulge are some of the most useful and important techniques for becoming a full-fledged, unstoppable, completely irresistible Bombshell. It sounds a little extreme, but believe me; these methods are so subtle and imperceptible that unless the man of your dreams has read this he won't know what hit him! I have a Signature Move that I will not divulge at any time to anyone but, dear Bombshell, I will tell you how to find your own and exactly how to use it!

Signature Move Starter Kit

Step One: The first thing you need to do is set up a video camera when you are able to spend a few moments alone. Alternately, a very close friend can be enlisted to help!

Step Two: Tape yourself doing everyday introductions but in different scenarios—like the business introduction, the first date introduction, or even introducing yourself to your local politician. I know you are skeptical about all of this, but I promise you I have a point!

Step Three: I want you to tape yourself having mock conversations—everything from getting your groceries to renting the latest video. Now, for your final video assignment, film yourself flirting or trying to persuade someone to see your point of view. That doesn't sound hard, does it? Well, let's take a look at these videos and study ourselves carefully.

Step Four: Begin with a quiet place and a glass of wine. Start to view your videos and, armed with a note pad, list all of the interesting little quirks that are unique to you and any mannerisms that jump out at you as things that you naturally do. When you are introducing yourself, do you look confident or are your eyes darting? Do you play with your hair when you flirt? How about when you are trying to be persuasive? What is the body language that you employ on a daily basis? Any of these unique, subtle gestures could easily be turned into your secret weapon; something that becomes a form of hypnosis, implemented silently and at a moment's notice. This can be a form of communication so powerful and so effective you will be shocked at what it can help you achieve!

Step Five: Once you have made this list it is time to start deciding which mannerisms you use when you are feeling your very best. Bombshell, it is so important to use association to build your confidence and give yourself that silent cue to be completely at ease in any situation. Your Signature Move will become your automatic, subconscious cue that you have an edge. Once you realize what the actions you make when you feel totally in your element are, you can start doing those very things when you are feeling particularly nervous or vulnerable to remind yourself that you have everything under control.

Step Six: Begin the process of making this second nature. Initially you may be aware of your Signature Move, but eventually it will kick into autopilot. This will be like your own Bombshell secret handshake; a little something extra to remind yourself of how special and unique you are as a woman. No one will be aware of your silent pep talk!

Kelly speaks:

I was finally interested in Mario; so much so that I was ready to pull out all the stops and get my man; so of course it was time to use my Signature Move. The problem was, I hadn't yet found mine and frankly I had seen The Bombshell Coach work magic with hers and knew I was ready to discover my own and put it to use! At first I was a little bit shy, even looking at family movies or tapes of the office party, but soon I noticed a pattern in my behaviour when it came to eating or drinking. I was actually surprised by how sexy I could look while I lingered over an hors d'oeuvre or how fascinated I was with the way I ran my little finger up the stem of my wine glass. Hence my Signature Move was born. I won't divulge the specifics of it now, but suffice it to say that Mario is like Pavlov's dog when I ring his proverbial bell with my Signature Move.

So Bombshell, have you found your move yet or are you having a little difficulty? If you are finding it hard, then it is time for a bit of help from the professionals who are available to help twenty-four hours a day—the stars! There are many reasons that the biggest stars are so successful. For one, they have a team of people watching them at all times ready to help, study and suggest. So, if you really can't find a move that you use naturally (which I find hard to believe), then as an absolute last resort, look around at celebrities or movie characters to find a movement that you think is interesting and that you think you could use yourself.

Kitten Moves Anyone?

This may sound strange to you, dear Bombshell, but bear with me and I'll explain how even the average house cat can be an amazing source of inspiration for those of you who have yet to find your Signature Move! What is it about cats that has fascinated mankind for centuries? Even the Pharaohs of ancient Egypt worshipped cats to the point of emulation. Well, maybe that's not such a bad idea: it seemed to work for Cleopatra! What I'm suggesting is to look around you and study symbols of beauty and grace that aren't on the covers of the latest magazines. Watch and see what makes the moves of a cat so graceful or the mannerisms of a kitten so irresistible. Then, I want you to see if you can apply any of that to your own, every day carriage.

This study of a cat can be applied to any animal you happen to be particularly fond of. I caution you, however, that it might be difficult to find graceful, attractive mannerisms in a bullfrog!

Serious-Secret-Man-Getting-Move

This tip should come with a disclaimer because once you use it, Bombshell, it's all over for the unsuspecting victim! Including this was a big decision since it is a secret I have held and utilized for years. I know I'm being dramatic, but sometimes it's hard to let go of these secret weapons, not to mention that all the men I've ever used these on will know that I had an unfair advantage over them. Here goes, but don't blame me when you have too many men and too little time.

Men love to feel powerful. They have been raised—generally speaking—to be strong and in control, and we Bombshells have a secret way of making them feel stronger and more powerful than the average woman.

Once you have an interest in a man and want to pursue him further, it is time to do the unthinkable—show him your ultra-feminine swoon, that Signature Move, and prepare yourself to get exactly what you're asking for!

Celeste speaks:

Kyle and I had been dating for a few months and I really liked him. Realizing that I could convey a fierce sense of independence, I welcomed the opportunity to show him how much I needed and valued his strong, masculine side. As we turned the corner we were forced to walk through a group of rather vocal guys who weren't shy about voicing their "admiration" for me. Now normally this wouldn't be something I was unable to handle but I quickly understood that this was a great time to let Kyle take care of me! I held on a little tighter to his hand and gave him my Signature Move to convey silently that I was a little nervous without having him go overboard. Kyle held me tight, pulled me closer and kissed me on the end of my nose when we were well past the "danger." This was a winning situation for all; I felt loved and protected and he realized that I needed him in that special way that a woman sometimes needs a man—if he's lucky. He got to play superhero and I got to play damsel in distress . . . now we just play happy couple!

To begin, this move is meant to convey a subtle nervousness in you, the poor smitten Bombshell. You will want to find a visual sign (a.k.a.: your Signature Move) to convey a sense of bashfulness, thus making you seem easier "prey" to the powerful hunk of a man before you! Are you noting my sarcasm Bombshell? Now, I know many different ways to convey this kind of vulnerability, but you have to discover what works most naturally for you. I am simply refusing to tell you what mine is in detail, however, I will suggest you try things like looking wide-eyed up at him and looking down bashfully, for if you looked any longer you simply might faint! If that Signature Move isn't the one for you, try, perhaps, tugging nervously on a delicate strand of freshly washed hair, only to be done in conjunction with direct eye contact strictly reserved for him. Do not break these rules if you intend to utilize this highly specialized Signature Move or he will think that everything makes you nervous.

We want to make sure that he knows this reaction is only a direct result of his powerful masculine energy!

> **Tip:** Notice that when you become more aware of your movements, you are able to refine them considerably and although a Bombshell is never contrived she is most certainly conscious of her ability to be noticed and make her point silently!

> **Remember:** This Signature Move is in no way intended to convey incompetence or inability to achieve; it is simply a way of restoring a man's sense of self in a world that so often affords them mixed messages.

The key to this kind of Signature Move for your man is to understand the basic instincts of men. I think it is safe to say that societal conditioning is such that the very nature of a man is to hunger for a sense of domination and potency. In the age of feminism, men might find that slightly elusive. So the Bombshell takes it upon herself to restore him to his former "caveman" glory days—okay maybe not quite to that degree, but close!

We Bombshells have no problem with our doors being opened and our chairs pulled out for us, and from my experience men enjoy doing these things for ladies. Who are we, or Gloria Steinem, to take it away from them?

For my own peace of mind I must tell you to use your powers for good, not evil, as I am not sharing this knowledge to be used against the general population. Certainly, all women at some point have felt that nervous excitement of attraction but the true Bombshell will chose to use this to her advantage instead of pretending to be cool, calm, and collected! Why not take that genuine "twitterpation" and use it as a subconscious way to convey an interest and simultaneously make him feel a little manlier? Take it from me, I know men can stroke a woman's ego for the purpose of getting closer to her, and so should we, but a Bombshell does it with stunning accuracy and impressive results.

Now this might seem unfair, but I know for a fact that men use all of their powers in order to win over a woman, so the true Bombshell will give him a little of his own medicine. By the way, this prescription really works! I'm sure many women will be unwilling to give this a try, thinking, in error, that this is some form of manipulation, but truth be told, this is more like a form of Bombshell hypnosis. Sounds good, doesn't it? What you are actually trying to do is simply convey your true and natural feelings in a way unlike most other women. You see, this is just one more example of how a true Bombshell is considerably different from her less creative cronies. We know how to take the feelings that make many women uneasy and channel them into a charming and reassuring gesture to benefit not only ourselves, but those we are interested in on a romantic level. Men don't like to be backed into an emotional corner where they are forced to give direct answers to direct questions. I have also come to believe that a feeling of superiority gives them that extra bit of confidence to make a move that they would otherwise have been afraid to make for fear of rejection.

If you are finding this "magic" difficult to believe in, just try it. In a very short time you will come to rely on this as part of your success in life. You will be able to use it as a powerful instrument in the art of persuasion. As Bombshells, we have mastered the art of gentle, but effective ways to persuade others to subscribe to our point of view.

That Signature Move In the Business World

As every good Bombshell knows, there are many different aspects to achieving success in the business community. Some people take self-confidence courses, others like to brush up on their public speaking skills, and some even learn a new language. Well, the Bombshell is certainly learning a new language today, but it is an inaudible and exclusive one that can often give a girl a major leg up in the world of high-powered executives. Remember, dear Bombshell, just because you might not be a top executive yet doesn't mean that you won't be—if that's on your agenda!

The language of your Signature Move will become second nature to you at some point, but you might have to fine tune it for the required results you are seeking in certain situations. Clearly, channeling your energy into a coy or nervous look is not the way to go in the middle of asking for a promotion or when meeting new clients. I strongly suggest that a distinct and unwavering air of confidence is the way to go with potential employers and associates. The key, Bombshell, is to find the small, barely detectable move that acts as your subconscious trigger to unleash your optimum negotiating and problem solving abilities; something that takes you immediately to your no nonsense, I-can-take-care-of-this kind of place.

This might be more difficult to find than your romantic Signature Move, although for some women, this one is easier. Just remember, dear Bombshell, we have a major advantage in life as in the last few decades we have been raised to be multi-faceted. That's right, unlike our male counterparts (as much as we love them), we have been raised to be everything from wives and mothers to emotionally evolved businesswomen! In some ways we are lucky to have so much societal pressure, so let's explore and expand on as many of these things as possible. This is why you might have to take some time to discover how your "move" can be conducive to your daily business.

Bearing in mind that your Signature Business Move is meant to give you an advantage that only you are aware of, your body language will be very important. Smiling is still paramount and the move should not be one that elicits a defensive reaction from those around you. Remember Bombshell, you'll get more with honey than you do with vinegar! Consider taping yourself again, perhaps a mock job interview or some other situation that you might face at some point. On tape, dress the part as well or you won't have the same business frame of mind. If you don't see anything on your tape that you feel translates well, then do the same research as before. Pay close attention to certain politicians or television journalists—chances are you will spot something that feels like you and then you can make it your own.

Barbara speaks:

Establishing a Signature Move for the business world was a challenge, but once I broke my business interactions down, my move was staring me in the face. My move is in two parts. First, I absolutely always wear high heels to important meetings to change my stature and highlight my confidence. The second part of my move is what seals the deal: when listening to those I am negotiating with, I hold my gold-tipped pen slightly over my heart. This is a great move because it is subtle: at any time I could be taking notes! This move is my automatic confidence builder and my trigger to be on high mental alert. This is my lucky charm and I believe it conveys a real sense of capability and readiness to do whatever necessary to get the job done—my way!

Using your Signature Move is always risk free because no one ever knows that you are doing it and this is why this little magic trick is one that the true Bombshell will always try and probably will always use!

The crucial element is to choose one that is very subtle and will become second nature. Once these things naturally occur based on your situation, it becomes a social four-wheel drive—always there when you need it to pull you through! This, with all of the other advice in the book, is hopefully used together, as they will be exponentially more effective when used together.

There is always something magical about little secrets. Knowing inside your Bombshell soul that you have something that is strictly yours, a soundless and powerful tool to be used by you automatically never to be consciously perceived by others is its own spell. This whole concept makes your Signature Move even more appealing, doesn't it? Well then, I suggest you keep that secret entirely to yourself. I advise you to revel in its secrecy. Hold it close to you, never revealing to anyone what it is. Not your best friend, not your boyfriend, and maybe not even your mother—although, my Mom thinks she knows mine! It should be something that you share only with your soul. Your sparkle will become more powerful and mysterious when you feel that extra bit mysterious, Bombshell.

"It is the inner TNT that over shadows any T and A"

"Women need to stop being search lights...turn that light inward and become the beacon for others"

"Do the same things to keep your partner as you did to get your partner"

CHAPTER ELEVEN

Find Him, Get Him, Keep Him . . .
If He's Worthy

CHAPTER ELEVEN
Find Him, Get Him, Keep Him . . .
If He's Worthy

Flirting is perhaps one of the most important skills a Bombshell will ever learn. While you must implement all of the elements to being a Bombshell, nothing will be more fun and exciting than learning how to effectively use your feminine wiles. Once you properly utilize the art of flirtation, you will use it every day to some degree. This gift is given to you directly from Venus herself and you will thank her one day, I promise. Upon realizing the fun and power it can provide you with, I know you will explode with a burst of womanly energy that will be central to maintaining your unwavering self-confidence and provide you with an amazing outlet for your feminine presence to be felt!

Learning the Basics

There are many secrets to flirting, but the fundamentals are easy—touch, talk, smile and gesture. Doesn't that sound easy? Ha! The key to successfully implementing these is to know the other fundamentals—who, how and where. Flirting can come with some inherent social dangers that we Bombshells try to avoid at all times. The main thing to remember is that once you truly embrace yourself as a woman you can begin to use flirting for fun and start to watch all the amazing side effects that come with it. I know that there are millions of single Bombshells longing to unleash the inner Blanche Deveraux lurking within. Perhaps you may not use it to that degree, but who knows? How far you take it is completely up to you as long as you remember that good taste and sensitivity are major ingredients to a successful flirtation, you can never go wrong!

Never underestimate the power of being a woman. The real challenge when it comes to flirting is establishing where the line of good taste lies. A Bombshell always does a beautiful job of toeing that line—while still wearing heels. For some women, flirting comes naturally, but for others, it takes much more effort to let go of fears harbored since the first day of grade eight. Being a flirt can release with a whole lot of horsepower, so I suggest that you hold on and enjoy the ride but take no prisoners Bombshell, you won't have time for any passengers on this ride!

Flirting for Fun

Flirting for fun can be the perfect opportunity to relax and let your inhibitions take a back seat. This is the best way to ease yourself into the position of becoming a flirt extraordinaire. Make it safe and begin with people you are already acquainted with, like the guy who fills up your water cooler or even an old boyfriend you have remained friends with.

> **Tip:** When you pick up your garments at the dry cleaners, take an extra split second look and say "Did you get contacts? Your eyes look amazing!" Don't wait for a response unless it is offered. Just smile brightly and walk out. Liberating, isn't it? The best part is that you probably made someone's day which is a crucial step in feeling like a Bombshell. Making a comment that will grab the interest of the receiver is the key to success here. But walking out before they have time to read to much into it is very important as well...leave 'em wanting more!

You see, when people feel special and appreciated, they will go that extra mile for you, dear Bombshell, which never hurts in life or love.

Flirting For Your Love Interest

Flirting to capture the man of your dreams is an age-old practice and it works. The Bombshell has her own subtle, or not so subtle, way of doing it. She never fails to implement whatever skills necessary to catch the attention of the one she really wants. The most distinctive thing about Bombshell flirting is that when used in conjunction with all of the other steps, a man can't help himself in her presence but will be totally unable to articulate quite why that is.

So, Bombshell, do you have the one in mind? Maybe you've seen him at the gym, or perhaps he works in the same office building as you. Wherever you see him, the techniques will remain the same.

Here are a few simple reminders to help you flirt successfully the next time you are out:

Reminder 1: Once you have him in your sights, go out of your way to say "hi" or make small talk. Even a few little words can be dripping with flirtation when executed properly. That means slowly but not like you are delivering a speech.

Reminder 2: Incorporate your Signature Move when flirting for the right date. Never ever forget your Signature Move as I can assure you that a love interest won't.

Reminder 3: When you smile at him, you want to give him direct and purposeful eye contact. When you do this, I actually want you to picture your positive energy flowing from you, straight into him. I assure you that men can feel the power from a woman who knows who she is and what she wants.

Reminder 4: Never underestimate the power of your confidence.

When you start the initial phases of casual contact, try to stand far enough away for him to admire you, but make sure you are close enough to lay a hand on his arm to help punctuate a sentence. Smile at him and let yourself be open to whatever energy he is putting forth. Believe it or not, this can be a very important mutual exchange, and all without stating your intentions. The Bombshell flirt will always walk the fine line with her interest, as she will remember that being slightly elusive is exceptionally attractive. Men really need to feel safe, but they definitely want to know that they are chasing something rare and valuable. I have always thought that in the initial stages of flirting, the good Bombshell knows to always end the conversation first, but not before a direct look into his eyes and a very sincere compliment. I think this leaves him aching for more of you while still thinking about the fact that you like his eyes. Always leave them wanting more, but make sure he has a sweet taste left in his mouth.

Do It Bombshell-style: Activity

Go to a gas station and get an attendee to fill up your tank. When you are paying, try taking an extra moment to make eye contact. Don't stare at him like a hungry dog, just give him that extra second to say "thank you" and look straight into his eyes when you say it. You have conveyed a genuine appreciation for the service and it will serve you well in the future. This is practicing in safety for you Bombshell because if you REALLY blow it you can always speed away!

When you first begin the Bombshell's dance of attraction, it is important to use your body language to show him your inner sparkle. Don't be afraid to shine as you should only take serious interest in a man who loves to watch a woman sparkle and shine anytime, anywhere. Don't forget to use your sense of humor as a tool for the ultimate in flirtation. I cannot stress to you how attractive it is when a man sees a woman with great wit and ease of laughter, how sexy it is to see a Bombshell laugh and enjoy herself right in front of a man she clearly enjoys in company and appearance. It is conveying your generosity of spirit that few women—who aren't Bombshells—possess. This confidence in yourself will become one of your best avenues to convey your willingness to give that sparkle to the man you are interested in. Remember, everyone likes others who are willing to share those special things in their lives, and the Bombshell's natural resources are endless and easily replenished.

Almost anything can be done in a flirtatious manner, so try things like a lingering handshake or a light touch as long as it is well-timed and appropriate.

When you are introduced to someone new, try both direct eye contact and a warm two-handed handshake. Couple this with a genuine, dazzling smile and you will have mastered the Bombshell triple play! Remember, you are not waiting for a reaction when you are flirting for fun. This is a very subtle and gentle form of flirting for the purpose of entertainment. You must make sure not to go overboard, as we don't want any misunderstandings pertaining to the Bombshell's intentions.

Flirting With the Man You Already Have

I am about to reveal some very personal and foolproof strategies to keep the man in your life interested in you and only you. Remember, if you give him enough to keep him on his toes, he will always wonder what is next. That should occupy him sufficiently for the next few decades—assuming you want to keep him that long!

Once you have established yourself in a happy, healthy relationship, it is time to seal the deal, Bombshell-style. Men are a bit like children in that they seem to need constant stimulation, so let's give it to them. We need to face the facts. If we aren't stimulating him then we leave room for someone else to do our job. I firmly believe that we have to do two things in this department—keep them wondering and make certain they are having fun with you. These things make you almost impossible to replace and with the specifics I'm about to give you, I promise he won't know what hit him. If you work to get a man you had better maintain that work to keep him; it's only fair!

Kelly speaks:

I had a special dinner planned for Mario one night and couldn't decide if I should serve soufflé or fresh fruit for dessert. Jacqueline's advice to me was to "serve up some freshly-shaved, bald pussy!" I was a little weary of the idea because it was something that in my forty-four years on the planet, I had never done. After some convincing, I decided to take Jacqueline's advice and go with the more "exotic" dessert. After dinner, when I served dessert, Mario was floored. He loved it. You see, he was expecting a romantic dinner, but the dessert was unlike any he had ever had. Now, Mario always revisits that experience just before he goes out of town on business. By the way, he was fifty-three years old and he had never seen a woman shorn completely bald. Clearly, I was his first and only Bombshell!

Have I scared you yet? Listen ladies, I'm telling you the things you really need to hear. You can modify them to suit your own situations, but these are the exciting things that most men lose sleep over. I can't explain this, but it seems that when women commit to a man they seem to think they can sit back and do nothing. Wrong!

If you have found a man who you love to be with, then work to keep him. I can assure you that by being a Bombshell you will rest easy knowing that he will be falling over himself trying to keep you, too. If we only continue the efforts to dazzle him like we do in the beginning, we will greatly increase our chances of living happily ever after.

One of the most difficult things for women to accept is that men are attracted to women who have let go of their insecurities. You should have released these nagging impediments way back in Chapter One! When you realize that self acceptance is the key to feeling sexy, then you can begin to plan some fun and unusual ways to showcase your talents. There is no bigger aphrodisiac than a woman who is unconditionally self-confident. I will tell you Bombshell—the woman who feels sexy, is sexy. Soon, you will start to become the sex kitten you always thought you could be and this will help you pull off the next few suggestions while modifying them into tricks that are uniquely yours.

Date night is by no means a new phenomenon, but when done Bombshell-style it makes the night unforgettable for both of you. Remember that this little teasing is not just fun for him, they are sure to make your life more interesting as well. Now, please be prepared as I am going to give you a great exercise to practice on your next date. This has a definite R-rating! The next dinner date you have with your significant other will be unlike any other if you follow my suggestion.

So, ladies, I assume you understand that the Bombshell approach to keeping him excited is a little unorthodox compared to some of your less ambitious friends, but that is the point. We revel in being unusual and taking a few calculated risks. I say calculated because these tips are Bombshell-tested and man approved.

Don't underestimate yourself and think that you can't do this sort of thing. Every true Bombshell is able to pull these things off. No pun intended! I admit, the first time might be a little frightening, but once you see the results, you will be much more likely to do it again.

I had an interesting conversation not long ago in which I explained to someone the importance of being flirtatious and spontaneous in a long-term relationship. I was stunned when this person said, "I suppose, but I don't want to have to play games like that in a relationship." I was shocked by this and quickly proceeded to remind the person that during courtship, people will often go to extraordinary efforts to entertain the opposite sex, even after just a few dates. Why, I asked, would you not put in at least that much effort for the one you have fallen in love with and committed your life to? My point, dear Bombshell, is that we should always try to employ the same sexy and entertaining moves to keep our man as we did to get our man. As a Bombshell, I know that if we really look at what our partner means to us, we will realize that giving them the efforts of the early days is the key to keeping the passion in the relationship. Maybe the mistake so many people make is looking for love much harder than looking for ways to keep it.

Barbara speaks:

We had settled in for dinner at a romantic restaurant and I excused myself to the ladies ' room just after we had finished our appetizers. When I got in there, I took my panties off from under my skirt and tucked them into the palm of my hand. I was a little bit nervous as I approached our table again, but as I sat down, I passed my panties under the table to my date while our eyes were locked. Once he realized what I had just done, the only words coming out of his mouth were "check please!"

Flirting Faux Pas

Even though we are becoming Bombshells, there are certain things that are not acceptable, no matter how glittery we are. Every once in a while the mood may strike and that inherent ability to be coquettish may surface when perhaps it should be suppressed. Yes, ladies, there are times that we must reign in our sparkle and behave ourselves, as we must always try to be demure when most necessary. I am obligated to tell you that flirting when misused, can get you into trouble, so make sure you are aware of your own actions and body language. We don't want the mailman to think he's being invited in for a nooner!

There are a few things that being a Bombshell will never change and one of those is being a lady at all times by trying to take other people into consideration. For these reasons, it is never okay to flirt with another woman's husband. This is just a waste of a Bombshell's talent and can serve no healthy or constructive purpose.

I don't care how cute he is, all of the Bombshell's friends' significant others are completely off limits. I have always been a "chicks before dicks" kind of woman, for as any good Bombshell knows, men will come and go, but a true and loyal friend is rare and priceless. Under no circumstance does a

Bombshell cross that line, and if by some terrible stroke of luck you find your best friend's new man attractive, avoid him at all costs. In this situation, there is no such thing as harmless flirtation and the risks are substantial. I don't think you have to stifle who you are as a woman, but certain men may try to take that a step too far and that is simply something the sisterhood will not tolerate.

Sometimes it's just a matter of being more aware of your mannerisms around that particular man and maintaining a certain sense of decorum so there are no misunderstandings. Besides, nothing is more repulsive to a Bombshell than to become a bad cliché!

It is also important to be sensitive to those who may take your innocent flirtations a little too seriously. Men who are newly single or divorced are much more vulnerable to the Bombshell's arsenal of feminine weapons. Unless you have a serious interest in this kind of man, it is very important to tread carefully in order for you not to hurt someone already in a difficult emotional place. A true Bombshell will know how to curb what may be a natural flirtation when required. In addition, generally speaking, those who are terribly wounded won't be the kind that will attract us on any level other than that of a compassionate friend.

Flirting is a powerful tool, Bombshell, so always remember that it is our responsibility to be aware of its consequences at all times.

"A true Bombshell will always leave those she meets hoping to see her again"

"Your appreciation for others will be the seed for a garden of Bombshell blooms!"

CHAPTER TWELVE:

Bombshells and the Company They Keep

CHAPTER TWELVE:
Bombshells and the Company They Keep

Now hear this Bombshell: I am about to tell you about the right people to know. Are you taking note? Every person—that's right, every person—you come in contact with on a daily basis can bestow upon you some gift of knowledge. I know you expect me to name off some grand list of the most important people out there, but I can only give you guidance about who can help you in social situations and life in general. But make no mistake about it, Bombshells are not self-serving social climbers and I won't, for even a moment, endorse being so. You see, the whole beauty behind the Bombshell philosophy is its care and embracing of oneself and others. I am not advocating that you become a human doormat with nice shoes, but I do believe whole-heartedly that there is a perfect balance to be struck.

One of the most satisfying things about being a full-fledged Bombshell is that people start to become inexplicably drawn to you. I can't fully convey to you the impact this will have on your life. It is just one of those things that you must experience to understand how magically it can change the way you live your every day life. This evolution will allow you to gain an appreciation for all kinds of people in many different capacities. Imagine taking average, mundane tasks and gaining positive and uplifting experiences, as well as spreading that positivity to those who are in contact with you. This is a win-win situation for everyone involved.

Every Day People Not to be Missed

The most important aspect of your interaction with people is to be friendly and open to who they are and the qualities they possess. So often we rush around doing our daily activities that we hardly recognize what may be an extraordinary efforts by people who are doing the best they can with the choices they have made in their own lives. For instance, I recently started going to a new laundry service (I realize that this is not the most glamorous example, but please bear with me). By my second visit to this dry cleaner,

I started to realize just how much pride the woman who served me there took in her work. She didn't own the shop and she wasn't working for a commission of any sort, but she had already done things like memorize my preferences and had my computer file up on the screen when she saw my car pull into the parking lot. This was very impressive as far as I was concerned and so I made a point to tell her what a fantastic job she was doing and let her know that all of her extra efforts were not going unnoticed. This started a conversation between the two of us and I soon learned that she had just been left by her ungrateful husband and that she had taken on this job so that she could feed her children. I was so inspired by her strength and optimism and she was so happy to be appreciated for her efforts! As an added bonus, she now takes extra care of my clothes and never forgets to hang my pants by the waist. If I'm in a hurry, I can just dash in, smile and wave at her, assured that she knows all of my information and will take complete care of me. I guess the point I am making here is that we, as Bombshells, should always watch for and acknowledge the extra efforts of others on a daily basis. We all have a story to tell and there is certainly always something we can learn from others. Telling someone about the things they do well is such a nice diversion from all of the possible negativity that we seem to endure every day.

Of course some people are easier to get to know than others, but there are no boundaries that the Bombshell cannot gracefully navigate. There will be times when you have to assess the situation on the fly and rely strictly on your own, firm foundation as a Bombshell. Once you get to a certain point in your own development you will be able to approach everything with complete confidence and know that you are capable of anything. The key to meeting people, from social acquaintances to possible business associates, is to exude your unwavering and innate personal warmth and power to get into their souls a little. Believe me Bombshell, when you master this art, they will want to know you as much, if not more, as you want to get to know them.

Breaking the Ice

At one of the first political events I attended, to I had a ball walking right up to anyone who looked remotely interesting and introducing myself in an attempt to test out what made my introductions most appealing and effective.

In business and political situations, there are a number of key things that a Bombshell must arm herself with if she wants to infiltrate a new circle of people or contacts. The first is that you must always display your warm, inviting smile, as this is the universal ammunition. Secondly, make sure you go in there with information on the interests of the group. Thirdly, take your great sense of humor because coupled with flashing your genuine smile, you will disarm them so greatly that you will sparkle even if you get caught at an event with no information on the cause or reason for the event. You will charm them senseless and acquire the details later! Remember dear Bombshell, when in doubt, smile, be kind, funny and charming—who can resist that?

The approach for business and politics can be varied according to your level of familiarity with the group, but one thing should remain constant in your introduction of yourself: a firm, two-handed handshake. This seems basic I am sure, but you would be amazed at the number of women who have no clue how to properly shake hands. I get more compliments on my handshake than you would imagine, so clearly this is something that is noticed on a regular basis. Now of course I have made this my own by doing it Bombshell-style which means holding on just a fraction of a second longer than anyone else. I always do this when meeting people I want to make an impression on, be they male or female, but never hold on to the point where the person you are meeting pulls away first. Your shake should always convey the warmth and self-assurance that is so Bombshell.

Don't think it will be easy to find your best Bombshell technique for introductions as it sometimes takes a few awkward moments to learn what makes you the most confident and successful when meeting new people. There are times when the best thing you can do is introduce yourself to someone who looks like they already know everyone else and explain that you are interested in the efforts of the organization and that this person looks like they really know the ropes. Not only will the flattery make them feel good, but the genuine and honest expression of needing a hand is something that ninety-nine percent of people respond to. Of course, to use your Bombshell ways with a clearly well-positioned person at any event is generally a good idea, as long as you choose one who isn't too involved with the coordination of the event you are attending. Otherwise, he or she may be a little too busy to take proper care of you and make the necessary introductions.

People to Help You Work the Room

If you are having trouble distinguishing the people who might make you feel more at ease, get a refreshment and take a moment to scan the room. The person who appears to be run off his or her feet will certainly not have time to walk you through the room and be your middle man, but do remember dear Bombshell, that after going to a few events and practicing, you won't even think twice about delicately breaking into a group and introducing yourself. When you spot someone with a friendly face moving with ease throughout the room then you know that this person is probably the one to approach. After introducing yourself you should always make sure that you clearly understand this individual's connection to the organization as you may very well be in the presence of the little-seen president of the company and the Bombshell always likes to be well-informed, thus avoiding stuffing her stiletto in her mouth!

If you don't like this "helping hand" method of introduction, then I suggest you watch for small groups and engage them in conversation that centers on them. You see, people love to impart knowledge and information, so when you ask questions pertaining to the event, you will be sure to get some great conversation out of them. Remember that when at all possible you will have some knowledge of whatever function you are attending. If this is a charity event, the successful Bombshell will have armed herself with sponsor knowledge and maybe even a few relevant statistics. If this is a private retirement party for a CEO or some other such soirée, then you should arrive with some information on the career of the executive or whoever the person being celebrated is. The worst case scenario is that you are taken to an event that you have no prior knowledge of, if this happens to you Bombshell, use whatever current events are happening as your back up—as long as you know what you are talking about. This is just one more reason for the Bombshell to be well-read and prepared to have an interesting opinion on hand.

So now that you have made your smooth and confident introduction, it is time to make sure that everyone you have met has no chance of forgetting you. Often, corporate and political functions can be dry as toast, but they are never so when a Bombshell is present! We have a way of bringing fun into almost every occasion while remaining at least dubiously appropriate. Keeping mind that walking the fine line is what will make all those you meet want to see you again—and soon. People tend to be at very least slightly intrigued by those who stand apart from the group in their desire to shine gracefully. As Bombshells, we like to keep our contacts both entertained and amazed by us at all times. Just when they think our personalities are only skin deep we will surprise them with enlightening wit and dazzle them with relevant insight.

When meeting people at any event, you will want to make certain you get a business card (and give them yours where appropriate) and if you had even more than a five-minute conversation with them, make sure you contact them the next day to let them know how lovely it was to have met them. Technological advances offer an alternative to phone calls for those who are a little bit shy, so send a short email that gets to the point quickly as the Bombshell never wants this gesture to be misconstrued as anything other than a genuine display of fine manners. People are generally very touched by such displays of etiquette and they are sure to remember you at the next function!

Intimate Social Gatherings

So many parties, so little time! Being the Bombshell that you are will often precipitate a packed party schedule. Some will, inevitably, be more fun than others but you can always make the best of any soirée if you bring your positive attitude and wear a fantastic outfit. When attending small or more intimate gatherings at someone's home or at a restaurant you can really enjoy the company and get to know people as long as you follow a few simple rules. First, always bring an appropriate gift for your host or hostess as this is the person who has kindly extended the invitation to you. By bringing a small, thoughtful token of appreciation you show both your host and the other guests that you believe in showing thanks to those who are kind enough to include you in their merriment.

> **Tip:** Bring a gift for your host that is a little out of the ordinary without going overboard, perhaps a board game to play later. Or, take something that is seasonal for a little bit of fun! Flowers of course, are always appreciated, but make sure that they are prearranged because your host will not have time to do it herself—there are other things to be taken care of.

Secondly, when you are going to an intimate gathering where you don't really know the group, try to wear an interesting piece of jewelry or clothing. When you wear something unusual you signal to people that you are approachable and gives them an opening for casual conversation. One colorful necklace or cool hat can be all it takes for everyone at the party to see that the jewelry isn't the only thing about you that sparkles. Keep in mind, dear Bombshell, that we want to be both interesting and unusual but not totally outrageous.

Keeping the conversation going can often be the task of the Bombshell and if you want to get to know these people better then you will want to make sure that they are all at ease with you. I suggest asking questions of them and make certain they understand that you are genuinely interested in their reply. Look them in the eyes and use your body language to convey your interest. Leaning forward and maintaining eye contact will make sure that they feel you are being attentive to what they have to say. A true Bombshell knows that every person she meets will have something different and interesting to share with her. When you are open to listening to what people say to you and you successfully convey this to them, they will forever be interested in sharing themselves with you and that is their gift to you!

The Most Sought After Dinner Reservations

Eating out Bombshell-style is one of the things that makes being sparkly so much fun. The key to always getting the best tables as well as scoring spectacular last-minute reservations, is introducing yourself appropriately. These introductions are not only fun but can go a long way to being treated like a mini celebrity which can be particularly useful when you have people in town you need to impress.

When you book your reservations, always use your first name so that you automatically form a sense of familiarity with the establishment. It will probably be refreshing for them to deal with someone who operates under no pretenses. If it is not your reservation, but say, that of a date or friend, then remember to introduce yourself directly and use your handshake Bombshell! The warmth of this initial contact will be a positive experience for both of you. I recommend asking to meet the chef or, better yet, ask the owner of the restaurant if he or she will take you back to meet the chef in the kitchen. I have never had an owner turn me down and the chefs love attention from an admirer of their talents. Make sure to tell them what you really loved about your dining experience and ask what they might recommend for dessert. This is truly their area of expertise and it is a Bombshell's talent to be able to convey true appreciation of their craft. Trust me when I say that restaurateurs all over the world will remember you always as the consummate Bombshell.

People Not Pawns

I want to be certain that I have made it clear that this is by no means a chapter on using people to get what you want from them, KINDNESS IS NOT CURRENCY! On the contrary Bombshell, it is about an appreciation for who they are and what they do, regardless of the level of glamour attached to their position. It is simply a side effect that when you express your genuine respect or admiration for someone, they tend to want to show you their very best and anyone who feels that they are doing whatever they do well will begin to sparkle themselves. If you take some glitter gel and rub it on your arm, do you notice that it is all over your house and kids in a matter of hours? Well Bombshell, you need to think of your own sparkle in the very same way. It is contagious and just by brushing some shine against people in everyday life you are able to share the kind of happiness you feel for yourself into the lives of others. It is so rewarding to watch people light up in your presence knowing that you can really make someone's day just by extending yourself to them on a sincere and open level.

CHAPTER THIRTEEN

Because Happiness is Contagious

CHAPTER THIRTEEN
Because Happiness is Contagious

Happiness. Sounds pretty simple, right? Well, if you are one of the lucky ones who naturally sees the glass as half full then you are well on your way to a very content existence. Always focusing on the positive and making the best out of less desirable situations seem to be easy things to do—or at least they are to me, but that's because this is second nature to me. I have programmed myself to see what good can come from a situation and a kind of positivity weaves its way through every aspect of my life. If finding the cashmere lining of the itchy burlap bag is appealing to you Bombshell, then keep reading.

Avoiding the Dark Thinkers

Remember that everything in life is a choice and that to choose to be happy above all else is a Bombshell imperative as long as your happiness is not established at the expense of others. They can participate in your glee but are not to be stepped on to get there. There are so many ways to build a positive infrastructure in your life dear Bombshell, so don't forget that you can have your own pep squad all the time if you open yourself to that possibility. It is important to realize that who and what you surround yourself with will go a long way in terms of how you feel about your life because those people and things are your world. Look at it this way, if you are doing your emotional laundry, do you really want to muddy the water with someone else's negativity? I don't think so Bombshell. Once you understand that, without exception, you choose the major players in your life and choose wisely when you are looking to build a winning team.

I know we have all had the misfortune of being exposed to the chronic complainer or the lost souls who have chosen to be victims in life instead of the victors. You may even have dated or married some of these characters, but hopefully you will begin to realize your power to choose what you expose yourself to.

In the free world we are afforded the choice to surround ourselves with goodness and light, so it always astounds me when women choose otherwise. Have you ever noticed how contagious laughter and enthusiasm can be? The old adage, "Laugh and the world laughs with you. Cry and you cry alone" is undeniably true, so when you meet a dark thinker, run!

The dark thinkers or "neg Nancys" as I have heard them called, are very easy to spot once you start keeping an eye out for them. They can come in many shapes and sizes, so don't ever be fooled by a pretty package. It is the little things that you will notice at first. They are often hypochondriacs who "discover" small, insignificant ailments that seem to plague them endlessly, thereby plaguing everyone around them. Or maybe they are the type to let small remarks slip when confronted with someone else's achievements: "Oh, she only got that promotion because she's always wearing short skirts." Small things at first, but once you start to see a pattern and have made the choice to rid your life of these people you need to cut ties with them as soon as is socially possible. People like this cannot be brought to the trough of happiness because they simply aren't programmed to drink. Do not, dear Bombshell, ever make the mistake of thinking that you can change these people as they have to do this kind of work by and for themselves. Besides, aren't you too busy changing your own life for the better? We may share our clothes, and possibly our accessories, but there is no extra soul to be doled out to those who are emotional bottomless pits.

Are you taking stock of those closest to you? Good! Granted some affiliations are harder to dissolve than others, but hey, you only see nasty Aunt Nell every three years and can just grin and bear her for the holidays. Now if you find yourself in the very unfortunate position of having a negative or toxic parent then I suggest a totally different tactic. Keeping in mind that my most recent idea of therapy is a great pair of high heels, I propose you keep your exposure to a minimum and augment the rest of your life with some super healthy, emotionally supportive friends—who have great taste in shoes!

I am not advocating bailing on anyone who is having a bad week, but I am saying that you should watch carefully for the warning signs of an imbalanced friendship or relationship. If you start to dread hearing from this person on a regular basis, then it is time for you to reassess the situation to see if this is a relationship that makes you fundamentally happy.

Girlfriend Warning Signs

As I told you in the beginning of the chapter, some of the people in your life may soon come to resent your newly uncovered Bombshell sparkle, so it is very important to watch out for any indications that some women you may consider friends might be less than thrilled to see your glamorous evolution. I hate to say it Bombshell, but there are many people in the world who subscribe to the nasty adage that "it is not that I should succeed but that my best friend fail," but the Bombshell and her cohorts would rather see everyone raised a level rather than swim in the sea of mediocrity. Unfortunately, this is not always the case.

I want you to think about whom you seek advice from on a regular basis and start to notice the different kinds of advice you receive from different sources. I know we all like to think that we have chosen our team in life well, but this study of the people around you may turn out to be more eye-opening than you think. For example, what if you went to your best friend and told her that you wanted to embark on a journey of self-improvement, both physically and mentally? What do you think her reaction might be? What I am sure you hope for would be an embrace with words of encouragement and offers of support in every way possible, right? Or, better still, an offer to take the journey with you as a companion in the search for the positive aspects of self-improvement and who will go the distance right beside you. Unrealistic? Perhaps for some, but not if you have chosen your life team carefully. If you feel you can approach the people closest to you and say, "Hey, I'm on my way to a better me" without being judged then you are on a good path. But what if you have people questioning your lofty ambitions and planting small seeds of doubt in your newly-planted Bombshell garden? The key is to recognize those seeds before they take root in your subconscious.

There are so many ways to undermine someone and sometimes they are so passive-aggressive that they can be missed entirely. Not by the astute Bombshell though! Anyone in your life who uses phrases like "What do you need to do that for?" or "I don't see the point, but go ahead," are the people you should be on the alert for. When my journey first began there were women in my life who I believed were my friends, but when it came down to their truest feelings, they just wanted me to be one of them, not the best me I that I could possibly be.

Any time someone around us achieves a personal milestone we invariably take stock of our own lives and for some this can be a frightening experience. It isn't that these people are necessarily bad, but look at it this way, if they aren't able to explore a world of bigger and better things for themselves, then how can they possibly encourage others to consider it? You see Bombshell, we are only capable of what we can conceive, so for some, the idea of stepping outside the safety of average is not something they will allow themselves to think about. This is probably because if they do, they will be forced to admit that in at least some aspects of their lives they have settled and to watch someone who was once like them become a fantastic, sparkling, dynamic creature makes them very uncomfortable because they may find that it punctuates their own lack of effort to improve.

I can tell you to watch out for these women, but you may still take a few emotional hits before you are able to weed these people out. There will be some who don't even know that they are negative, toxic human beings, but we can identify that they are clearly not looking to better themselves and would be unable to support our hunt for the inner Bombshell. There will also be a few who want to be near you to suck a little of your positivity and goodness. Do not feed the people who are not willing to nurture you in some way as well and only want to spend time with you so that they can ride the tidal wave of goodness that you have created for yourself. They are the ones who will want to go out with you to siphon off some of the attention they see you getting or to perhaps feel the sparkle vicariously through you instead of doing the work themselves. Now don't get me wrong, I am a huge advocate of sharing the shine that is inherently Bombshell, but we have to be careful not to throw pearls before swine.

I remember my best friend silently watching my evolution. She never put me down or told me I was wasting my time, but she was not yet ready to take the journey herself until something moved her one day and she realized that this kind of transformation could be taught. She came to me and asked how she could better herself and find her own sparkle. I have always admired her for her strength of character because it takes so much for a woman to approach her friend in this way as opposed to being jealous or intimidated by her. So I took her hand and we walked the road together, supporting one another when needed, but loving and accepting all the time. She was clearly part of my winning team and I a part of hers. Her sparkle is all her own, although she attributes the discovery of it to me; it is special and unique to her and no less strong or beautiful than my own. The one unshakeable similarity is that we both chose to find it and gave ourselves permission to enjoy it.

Sadly, I have also had experiences where I was unable to clearly see the ulterior motives of so-called friends. I have since adopted the "Fool me once, shame on you. Fool me twice, shame on me" motto. I had a woman in my life who touted herself to be a loyal and dedicated friend, but I learned the hard way that this person was really an ill-intentioned and jealous woman who had no clue that it was what I was wearing on the inside that made me beautiful not the latest style as she led herself to believe. Although imitation is the sincerest form of flattery, she soon realized (after copying every outfit in my wardrobe) that nothing was changing in her life, no matter how she tried to disguise herself as a Bombshell on the outside. Her own lack of self-esteem was her ultimate undoing and she eventually got angry and bitter, showing her true colors (she certainly was green). Jealousy is a direct result of someone's unhappiness with themselves and their unwillingness to change it. You can wrap yourself in the most beautiful ribbons and bows but eventually the muddy water will seep through the packaging and expose the fact that you haven't made yourself beautiful where it really counts. Anyone who insinuates that your beauty is a result of what you have done to yourself externally is gravely mistaken, Bombshell!

Don't make excuses for these people. If they are not reaching for their goals, it is generally due to their own volition and nothing more. By no means am I saying that you should cut from your life those who don't aspire to more, but I am certainly saying that you should avoid spending time with those who clearly don't support you or start to treat you differently (negatively) as you become a happier, more confident woman. Small, cutting remarks passed off as jokes are surefire ways to tell that these people are unhappy within themselves and that you may very well be the misplaced target of their personal disappointment and frustration. "She thinks she's so great since she started taking care of herself" or "Oh, she's too good for us now that she's gotten that promotion"; these kinds of remarks are incredibly toxic and serve no purpose in the happy, glamorous world of the Bombshell. Remember, when you are swimming to the surface of self-improvement, there is no point in wearing ankle weights.

What do you do to keep your own positive frame of mind in the face of people like these? Well, once you have begun your journey to Bombshellhood you will have plenty to be glad about, but in the meantime you have to make the conscious choice to look only at the wonderful ways in which you have evolved and even the ways in which your own happiness affects those around you. If you need some extra encouragement then take out the "before" pictures of yourself from your Beauty File and list the little (and not so little) ways in which you can see your improvements. We all have days when we don't feel like movie stars, but it is precisely these times when your winning team will be so important, as they will step in and give you the boost of encouragement that everyone requires from time to time.

Energy Drainers

I always tell people to be aware of how they feel after spending time with different people that they have regular interactions with. This is an excellent way to gauge the kind of person that they are and the ultimate impact they will have on your life. I am quick to warn women about the people who seem to suck the life force out of your soul; these are the ones who are trying to ride the wave of your energy and end up leaving you feeling a little more depleted than you should. I know you know the sort of person I am talking about, but have you ever stopped to notice the effects of your affiliation with them on your being? It is easy to let these people slip in under your radar because we Bombshells can often be suckers for those who come across as needing us. Beware. Giving generously is certainly a Bombshell quality but be conscious of feeling a lack in mutual exchange of encouragement.

Does Changing You Mean Changing Your Man?

Well Bombshell, this can be a tough issue to contend with, even for the most seasoned graduate. Finding the solution to this question lies squarely on your shoulders, so it's a good thing you have been working out! The above rules for friends and associates should always be applied to your intimate relationships and maybe even more astringently. Why, you may ask, should we be harder on our man than our other relationships? The answer is simple: once you are in an intimate relationship you have established the loan of a part of yourself emotionally and in return have received a part of that man for yourself, and you therefore make yourself a little bit vulnerable. This is great if you have chosen him carefully, but what if you let him in by default and now that you are becoming everything you always wanted, you realize that there may be some serious issues on the horizon?

When you embark on this journey you may be single and your relationship status may be part of the reason you are on this trip. If this is your motivation, you must remember that the positive steps that you make are for your benefit only. Once you do this you know the foundation is based solely on motivations and inspirations that are meant to affect the self alone. Nothing that you own in your soul can ever be taken from you dear Bombshell. That being said, let's get back to the man in your life. If you are single at the outset, your progress will ensure that you have developed some sense of what you want out of life and this makes you far better prepared to make the choice of a great partner to join your life.

The point I want to impress upon you is that a healthy, happy woman will generally make better choices, for she will know that she deserves to be treated well, respected, loved and maybe even somewhat revered. We are, after all, Bombshells.

On the other hand, what if you begin this process and your long-time boyfriend, lover or husband does not (whether he says so outright or not) support you in your quest to improve your self? What do you do? How do you handle this situation? You clearly love him very much but his resistance to your rising self-esteem and confidence are off-putting; this is problematic. First things first: if you chose this person at a low point in your life, during a time when you know that many of your decisions were questionable, then this is definitely something you will want to address because your change in motivations can hugely change your relationship. I mean, if you weren't able to properly decide on being the very best you could, do you really think you were able to choose a partner who would encourage you to achieve greatness? Probably not, but that's not to say that there is no hope, no possibility it just may be a little more difficult.

When you start the process of embracing yourself as a woman he may start to notice right away. The hair, your personal upkeep and other visual clues will probably get his attention. After he realizes that you are not cheating on him, he may react in one (or more) of many different ways. He may start to say things that will give you clues as to how he will handle your transition and keep track of these ladies because you will need to know if he is going to be the one to prop you up or push you down. Do not underestimate the power of these clues and don't ignore anything that will show you his subconscious thoughts and feelings. I once dated a man who became more and more frightened of losing me, so he started making little remarks in an attempt to subtly undermine my self-esteem while trying to make himself feel better. He would say things when we were on our way out at night like "I hope you didn't pay a lot for that bag" or "Isn't that shirt a little bit small for you?" These remarks were clearly feeble and transparent attempts to make me feel less than worthy. I don't think he was saying these things for any reason other than to try and dull my shine a little. How sad for him, but how lucky for me because I, as a Bombshell, knew immediately what this was all about and it only reinforced my feelings of self-satisfaction, as I must have looked darn good for him to feel insecure enough to make comments like those. Don't let remarks like these get to you—just remember the source and keep your eyes open. Also beware if you are on a new workout regime and he is bringing you Häagen-Dazs or if he is rushing you while you are trying to get ready to go to work in the morning telling you that "you look fine" and asking questions like, "What do you need make up for? It's only work." These are some serious red flags. On the other hand, if he is going to the effort of making you low-fat smoothies and is telling you how proud he is of your quest to become a happier and healthier woman, make sure to appreciate the support because this could be a serious prospect for a winning life partner.

I have seen so many spectacular women guilted or manipulated into abandoning their journey to Bombshellhood partway. How tragic it is to see them wither away into obscurity just when their goals were finally becoming attainable. Don't let go dear Bombshell, and don't hang on to anyone who wants you to be less than mind-blowing, head-turning and stunning both inside and out (for every Bombshell knows that you can't have one without the other—at least not for very long). Never let this transformation be touted as selfish because the reality is that the better you become, the more you can give back to those who love you and life itself. This can't be bad. Even if some people are afraid of that personal empowerment, it is only because they can identify a lack of that quality in themselves.

Once the man in your life comes to realize that you are standing out in the crowd, becoming more and more confident in yourself and watching you achieve multiple goals, he may be inspired to his own greatness.

What is it that may be motivating him to keep you tied to your former mediocrity? Why wouldn't he want a woman who is beautiful and sparkly? Well, any of his insecurities will come to the surface once he realizes that you are really determined to reach your full potential as a woman and are making no apologies for it. So, dear Bombshell, you have several options and your choice will depend on your level of attachment to your man. You can calm his fears and invite him to take the journey with you, or you may end up feeling that you are outgrowing him and that you need to move on. Do try and understand that if someone put a million dollar diamond in your hand, you would be looking over your shoulder all the time to make sure that there was no one looking to steal it, but by the time you find your inner facets the Hope Diamond will have nothing on you and he won't be able to keep you in a safe!

That being said, I have met so many insecure men, who, upon realizing the value of the Bombshell in their life, attempted to smother her. They would suggest staying in more or that perhaps she did not get "all dolled up" just to go out for dinner. Then, if the signs weren't caught early enough, it may have progressed to even more outward, inappropriate remarks. Slowly but surely some men will try to build an emotional and social cage around their Bombshell that is comprised only of their own fears and insecurities.

If you choose to walk together on this journey, you must be the loving, accepting and encouraging partner that you expect him to be. All Bombshells know that a happy life is not a one way street. We want to share all of the positivity we can as this is a way to strengthen and improve both of you simultaneously. Talk about a mutually beneficial situation! This is what Bombshells love: sharing and inspiring everyone we meet to somehow see a bit of a sparkle in themselves.

You must remember that as he makes strides in his personal improvement, you may see women looking at him more often or that his presence is much stronger and you need to make certain that you do not perceive this as threatening. Your newly acquired self-image should be such that no matter how wonderful he becomes, you know that you deserve him and that you have inspired each other and have become closer in the process.

The Relationship File

What will you do if you feel as though you may be in a rut that you don't know how to get out of? What if you feel a strong bond with someone but become increasingly aware that this probably isn't the right man for you? Well Bombshell, just as you have been keeping a Beauty File, you will want to keep a Relationship File. You can either do this in your head, or you can actually start writing it down—just be sure that he won't be going through your panty drawer!

What are the long-term goals of your relationship? Have you ever even thought about where you two will emotionally be in ten years? I think it is so strange that most of us plan our vacations further in advance than our love lives. So many of us have five-year career plans but ignore the planning of the soul. I think it's time to change that and pay more attention to your long-term love goals. If you see yourself with someone (which you may or may not), what will be the things you deem non-negotiable? Take note of the sort of person you expect to have in your life at that point. Is he even a shadow of the person you are currently with or does he in any way resemble the men you choose to date? If he doesn't, you might need to reconsider the time that you are potentially wasting. I mean think about it Bombshell, if you want to be a doctor, do you go to school for exotic dancing? Probably not. Every step you take in life should be one in the direction of your ultimate goals and you can even take these steps in four-inch heels!

Have you decided what you need to be happy in the future? Good. Now start to explore what it is that your man sees for himself in five or ten years. Don't even attempt to sit him down for the Bombshell Inquisition, but start to take note of the things he says and his reactions to the things you express about your own goals. If you can't wait to own a home and start a family and he is thinking about traveling the world and volunteering for Greenpeace, then the positions you aspire to in your lives will take you off separately. Don't be mislead by this and don't think you can change his mind. It seems so simple for me to tell you to look at his aspirations as opposed to yours but so many women get caught in the web of maybes. "Maybe he'll see it my way in time." Maybe not. Then, before you know it you have given away one of the most valuable things in your life: time.

This theory applies to all of those occupying some amount of your emotional real estate. Take the control that you need and understand that you—and only you—are making the draft picks for your life team. You have a life to build for yourself and it is okay to choose the best of the best to be your offense and defense through your life. The same will apply to you because once you allow yourself to explode into the brilliance that inhabits you, it will be easy for others to covet you for their winning team. Remember how nice it was to be picked first for the team? That's what you want now, too.

Unless you have been kidnapped and forcibly confined, then you have no reason to feel helplessly trapped in an unhealthy relationship of any kind. Whether we refer to a husband or boyfriend or that "friend" who likes to say discouraging things, any person occupying time in your life is there based on your own choice. Tell those that you love that you expect to be treated with love, support and respect so that you are clear about the boundaries of the relationships you nurture. Fill your file with any information that you think will help you to make some of the difficult choices you may face.

Don't Be Afraid to Walk Away

Sometimes in life—even in the life of a Bombshell—we have to steel ourselves for the possibility that even though we may love someone, we have to let them go. This may not be a permanent release, but we need to be prepared for the reality that we may find ourselves in a situation that can't be made to work. Make sure to stand back and be confident that you have given the situation a fair chance and confirm that you have taken full responsibility for your part and efforts in the relationship (friendship or otherwise). Ask yourself: "Have I listened to this person and effectively communicated my expectations to this person?" If you can honestly admit that you feel good about your role in the relationship, but it isn't making you feel as though it is a healthy, mutual relationship, then you may want to step back. A Bombshell is able to walk away when she needs to as she knows her self-worth and what she has to offer. But don't be bluffing ladies. When you walk away, be prepared for it to be final. If you are ever in doubt, make a list of the issues that are prompting you to disengage.

Sometimes we tend to forget the bad things and this is especially true for those of us who tend to be positive thinkers. Most importantly, don't be afraid to give yourself permission to make the choices that are in your best interest so that you are always providing yourself with the best opportunity to shine and be happy.

Every winning team has a goal, a clear desire to come together for the good of all involved. Your life team should be no exception dear Bombshell— we are only as strong as our weakest link. I have very little sympathy for those who blame their life's shortcomings on others because as I have proven, we decide, we choose and we allow. If it isn't good in your life, get rid of it. I can promise you that life will hand you enough challenges that you can't control, so make sure that you are managing the things you can to your own benefit.

"You can feel someone without touching them, you can keep someone without holding on tight and you can always remain a Bombshell by showing without saying"

"It is her way that captivates; the warmth and the openness and what one can draw from her effortlessly"

CHAPTER FOURTEEN

Keeping the Faith and Giving it Back

CHAPTER FOURTEEN
Keeping the Faith and Giving it Back

In a world full of chaos and tragedy, it is sometimes hard to stay focused on all of the wonderful things about our lives and humanity in general. I know that at some point, everyone will look at their lives and the unrest in the world wondering what will become of society in general and those we love. Bombshells are not at all impervious to the strife of daily living, but we have developed a strong team and a storehouse of happiness to draw on at any time. It will be this reserve that will have the Bombshells of the world spouting sincere optimism while the rest of the population will be up in arms.

Faith in ourselves, dear Bombshell, is where we differ from all other women on the planet. The small setbacks and disappointments that can make others lay down crying after finishing two bags of cookies will have little effect on us. When you have adopted the mentality of the true Bombshell everything will appear brighter and better and easier to put into perspective. Our emotional faith comes directly from what we have discovered about ourselves as women and knowing that this strength is ours and is built on our own gifts, we possess a faith that is not to be taken from us because we have done the work to see our own power. It is those who draw their strength from others who need to be concerned because any power source that you draw from other than your own soul can be shut off without your consent in the blink of an eye. Rely on who you are and the abilities you have cultivated and know that these cannot be taken from you. We aren't made of armor, but we are so confident in our strength and resilience that we accept any challenges and know that we can emerge unscathed, and likely, well-manicured!

Once you fulfill your quest for a winning team in your life, you will come to know that your life is yours to direct as you desire. The self-respect and direction you have will make keeping the faith easier for you in a way that those who have not embraced themselves cannot. You see when you know and love all of yourself you shorten the distance to accepting yourself. Acknowledging your faults and flaws will allow you to go through life with nothing to hide. If you say to the world, "Hey, I'm not perfect, but I love me anyway," somehow the world will love you right back. People around you will have more faith in you and you will become stronger and more spectacular by the moment. So many women are afraid to admit that they are flawed, be it physical or emotional; they begin to revolve around hiding the part of themselves they dislike so much that they lose their focus on all of their wonderful and sparkling traits. Once you focus on something, you feed it and afford it a power over you and your life, so why not choose to focus on those things that you have absolute faith in? If you are working on being a better public speaker, but you are an amazing singer, then allow your singing to be your focus while simultaneously working on your other, less well-perfected traits. It's more than okay for you to say to the world, "Hey, I may not be a size two, but I sure am a happy and healthy size twelve." Acknowledgement will allow you the faith you need to tackle things without letting them be turned against you. You maintain a faith in your special qualities and lean on those a little when tackling other, more challenging personal goals.

The faith you have in yourself as a woman can become a tool for your inspiration of others and that will perpetuate the cycle of happiness. You will find that it is exactly this inspiration of others that will come back to you and hold your hand in times when you may be feeling a little bit drained, or like you are lacking some inspiration of your own—this is the life team I spoke of earlier. The faith you inspire in your circle of friends will be the same reserve that you can draw from, as we all need the invigoration of others at times. The Bombshell is no island, but she will create a population of loving, sparkly support that won't let her down, just as she will provide ample faith to others.

You will have bad days Bombshell. Sometimes they will be the things you can remedy and sometimes not, but what we can always do is control our reactions to these situations. The way we deal with a bad situation or some awful news can, to a huge degree, lessen the stress and pain of a terrible time. If you are dealing with something you don't want to talk about, then throw on one of your safety outfits and go out and find people to be nice to. This may sound unusual, but trust me, when you extend kindness to anyone, even strangers, you begin to restore your faith and energy to face whatever situation you have temporarily put out of your mind. Leave a wake of your glitter wherever you go and the reflection alone should be enough to brighten your own day. Kindness and happiness are infectious, so to spread them is to experience them and restore your faith in their power.

So much of the Bombshell's power comes from faith and belief in the greater good and what that goodness is capable of accomplishing for all those touched by it.

So when you go out in search of good deeds, make sure you do them for the sake of goodwill; not everyone will smile back and certainly not everyone will express gratitude, but you own those good deeds and they are yours to feel proud of. This exercise in bolstering your faith will be good practice for almost all of the Bombshell teachings. The faith you have in yourself and the team that you've built should be enough to cope with anything life can throw at you. Don't forget to rely on those you love. Not only is it nice for them to know that you need them, but it illustrates to them that they are an active part of your life team and this will make them feel as special as you know them to be. It isn't enough to rely on them, but when they have done something to give you a boost, the true Bombshell knows it is more than appropriate to make a big deal of their efforts.

Rally the Troops!

I find it uplifting to have Bombshell get-togethers sometimes. It can be so easy to let months and even years slip by without so much as a martini (or not so teeny) lunch. How many times have you stopped to address the lack of time you've devoted to nurturing your support system in life? We all try to make time but the true Bombshell doesn't just try, she does! Instead of making excuses start to make the phone calls you've been putting off, or better still, make invitations for a little soirée to reconnect with all the people you keep as friends. And don't forget to invite your moms, sisters and daughters to join.

When you finally get everyone to agree on a night, it is time to decide where to go and what to do. You could easily go to someone's house and relax, but wouldn't a fun outing be nice? The creation of memories will make beautiful scenery for the illustration of your lives together, so make them fun and enjoyable to look back on. Do something out of the ordinary like renting a private karaoke room. Sounds corny, I know, but I'll tell you, it's a fun and inexpensive way to have a great laugh with people you love. Knowing, as Bombshells do, that laughter is good for the soul, you will find this to be a wonderful evening filled with stories to recall. These are the kinds of things that keep people fresh and fun; the kind of things that one wouldn't normally do, but once you do, you realize the joy in feeling just a little bit silly sometimes. There is a reason childhood times were so free and easy— we didn't worry so much about being wacky.

Something about your newfound freedom of self-acceptance will make those times of whimsy much more abundant in your life and they will seem a more natural and healthy process. Imagine how sad life is for people who think that getting older means becoming more staunch and rigid. The true Bombshell knows that getting older means becoming smart enough to enjoy every wicked moment. Leaving behind the artful dance of childhood does not mean forgetting the steps.

Don't underestimate the bonding times you share with your friends and family because if you have chosen well, you will create a wealth of endless love and support that will carry through any situation life may toss your way. The building of this emotionally supportive structure should be beneficial to all those fortunate enough to be on this winning team and the give and take of positive energy and genuine encouragement will be a gift to be enjoyed forever. Laugh with each other, at each other (in a nice way) and at yourself and soon you will find that the joys of life remain at the surface so that you can enjoy them continuously. A generosity of spirit can often be gauged by one's willingness to enjoy the humor in life. There are those who really don't realize the power of a belly-rolling, cheek-aching laugh and are they ever missing out!

Reaching Beyond to Remember Your Strength

If time has gone by and you find you have gone stale, then it is time to make your life list and systematically do one thing on it every month. I am not talking about going to the gym or getting your hair cut because those things are already being taken care of. What I am talking about is a list of things that will take you beyond what you believe to be your limitations, like flying trapeze lessons or a trip to an exotic place all by yourself. It doesn't matter how old you are or what your mindset is, every Bombshell knows the value of doing the things that challenge her as a person.

Celeste speaks:

Jacqueline asked me what I most wanted to do for myself and it took a lot of thought, but I told her that I wanted to skydive. It was something I had wanted to do for a long time, but had been weary of actually trying it because of my children—I wanted them to be raised right. When I shared my goal with them (at Jacqueline's suggestion) my sons were so excited for me that they were bragging to their friends and my daughter exclaimed how proud she was that I was actually doing something for me. I seized the moment and lived my life for me, and in the process I learned that I am rearing my children right—they are becoming courageous and dynamic individuals by following my lead.

Understand Bombshell, that stepping outside of yourself and your comfort zone will afford you the opportunity of showing your kids and those around you that you are always willing to learn and take risks the way we expect them to do on a regular basis. It gives them the chance to feel how rewarding it is to be part of a winning team and shows them how important it is to be supportive of each other's goals. A Bombshell should always be willing to show those she loves how to be happy for another's achievements and the joy that it brings for everyone who supported and encouraged the efforts of the other. This will renew your faith in yourself and remind you of the wonderful creature you are. Challenging yourself is sometimes all it takes to give you back the faith in your abilities as a woman and as a Bombshell.

CHAPTER FIFTEEN:

Showing 'Em What You've Got

CHAPTER FIFTEEN:
Showing 'Em What You've Got

So much of our energy as women is locked up tightly within us, waiting and wanting to beam, but unless we give ourselves permission to shine we will simply be reflecting our goodness and positivity inwards which doesn't do anyone any good. The gifts that we have are meant to be shared with those around us. It gives the energy we already have a kind of unstoppable momentum that will perpetuate itself for a lifetime and will change every move you make once you understand it and embrace it. Only by the projection of this energy will you be able to share who you are with all those you come into contact with; it will allow you to change and achieve things in your life that you never realized were in your complete control.

Getting Started

There are a few key things to recognize when it comes to your own energy and power that must be addressed before you can fully release what you have been (perhaps inadvertently) keeping in your emotional safe. As a Bombshell you will be able to take stock of your internal assets and decide on the things that you really cherish about yourself as a woman. What I am about to do is show you how to transfer those assets into an energy that translates to all those you come into contact with, an energy and an air that is unique to you and that can be experienced by others without the spoken word. This may sound hard to believe but once you liberate your feminine spirit, it will take you over and make it easy to be noticed and admired for the power of your soul. We have become a society that hoards its energy and feels it is simply self-defense to keep ourselves emotionally unavailable, but the truth is that this is like having a tank of gas that never dwindles, but refusing to drive. Bombshells love to drive, so let's tap into this reserve!

There are a million different ways to explore your personal energy and come to feel this within yourself, but one thing remains consistent: in order to really unlock yourself, you must be willing and able to share this energy with others. I know so many women who have been raised to protect themselves emotionally, not realizing that protecting yourself and caging your spirit are two separate things. Once you understand the strength of spirit you possess, you embrace the idea of sharing it as just one more facet of your being that can be utilized however you choose. Your energy will flow through you and you will come to understand that its beauty, sparkle and endlessness are most of the protection your soul will require. Those with a dark or negative energy are generally frightened off by the brilliance of a woman who has fully developed her positive energy. It's rather a catch-22: those who are afraid to expose their energy seemingly have none and thus attract people who are likely to walk all over them (even when they are wearing expensive shoes!). You want to visualize yourself as a sort of lighthouse and once you have found the light within yourself, you must begin to emit this light in all aspects of your life. Remember though, this is not a search light because by this point you will already have done the work to find out who you are. This is a light to let others see who and where you are in your life, a light that attracts people who recognize its power and a beam that frightens off those who don't understand what it is. You become a beacon, attracting goodness.

Your palpable energy is like the DNA of your soul, completely unlike any other woman's and so telling about your emotional make-up. This is why it is imperative that you really understand all of your goodness and power so that everyone around you gets an accurate, albeit silent, portrayal of the Bombshell you have become. The work you must do to unbind yourself from the trappings of societal teachings will quite probably be extensive and educational. Look at it like going through an old drawer of keepsakes; you marvel at the things you find and can't imagine how you forgot so many amazing and special things about yourself. Take inventory of the moments in time when you saw glimpses of the soul you have been hiding for so long, mistakenly believing it was for your protection. It is this inventory that will remind you of the woman you are because often in everyday life we are so wrapped up in being lovers or mothers that we lose touch with ourselves as women.

When you realize that this resource is one that will never be tapped out, you will start to be able to spend and invest it wisely. You see, when you give something so valuable, it becomes a form of investment.

Yes, there is a certain amount of risk involved, but the return on your emotional investment will be greater than you ever imagined and the fact that you can never run out of your sparkle and personal gifts makes this an easy decision. You only stand to become a stronger, more stable and more beautiful Bombshell once you begin to release the power of your energy and share it with others.

An Observation

I once went shopping with an older woman I had known a short time, but her observations were so honest and profound that I feel I need to share them with you. I was walking slightly ahead of her as we both had children in tow and went about a fairly routine trip to the mall. When we got home and were sitting together with friends, she broke her afternoon of relative silence and said,

> It was the most amazing thing. I thought it was just men who would look at her but it was everyone—men, women, children, the elderly. They all just seemed to pause and watch her pass. This is not a case of a woman parading her sexuality because she was wearing terry cloth pants and a t-shirt! They just look because she compels them to.

Now I knew this already but to have someone who hardly knows me be converted from "Must be a blonde thing" to "Must be more than that" was a really nice validation for me. This was also a good indication to me that I am still allowing my positive energy to precede me and that I'm still doing it in a way that people can see and feel without ever making a sound or causing an embarrassing scene. It is my own, natural, free-flowing energy that has become my trademark as a woman and that I like to think leaves a wake of good feelings behind me. This is a Bombshell not willing to keep her energy to herself and making no apologies to those who are afraid of her power. A power that resides in every person on the planet; it is a superpower that society seems to be unwilling to acknowledge. This is absurd to me, rather like having a bank account full of money and not wanting to spend any, even knowing that it will be replenished automatically. Start withdrawing some of that energy Bombshell, and learn how to share it with those around you.

Visualize Your Color

What is your favorite color? If you had to name yourself after a certain color, what would it be? My color is and always has been blue. I am not talking about a color to wear all the time or to paint your house in, but a color that you feel is a reflection of your inner self. Maybe this color is one that you would never wear or even paint your toes, but it is one that you feel would be the color of your own emotional ocean. This will be like the tail of your comet, the wake of your energy and I want you to picture the color of your energy being left behind like fairy dust. Don't stop visualizing this energy leaving you until it becomes absolute habit, second nature. This is such a crucial part of the Bombshell you are becoming and is something that will both bring and spread joy. This is a situation in which you cannot lose.

Once you decide on the color that you feel represents you best, try to explain to yourself why you chose this color. This is important as it will be helpful in unlocking the things that you most value about yourself. I have always used blue because to me, it symbolizes happiness with calm but can be infused with an almost ethereal vibrancy and seems to be uplifting in a way that makes me feel safe and warm. This showed me that I value my ability to share goodness and make others feel safe and loved. I take these strengths and build on those as part of my personal energy because the things that we most value about ourselves are those which we can most rely on. For some women, red may be a better choice. Some Bombshells have chosen it for its powerful, fearless symbolism. Others chose shades of green for a strong sense of hope and nurturing. Whatever the color, make it your own shade so that you can use it to visualize the sharing of your gifts.

Eye contact is like a direct passage of energy from one person to another, almost like high-speed internet for the soul; only this can be deeply moving and have in impact on another with just a brief glance. Knowing this makes the Bombshell very effective in transferring a part of her energy directly into another without so much as the touch of her hand. When you make direct eye contact (as we addressed earlier in the book) with anyone you are automatically being taken more seriously and will command an instant respect. This is one of the essential tools to communicate an unobstructed view of your goodness and shine to those around you. People are often much less afraid when they realize they have a clear view ahead and this view is the best way to afford them a splash of your color!

Take this and begin applying it to your daily life, to every person you walk by and in your everyday dealings, look people in the eye and allow them to see your colorful energy. You will come to notice how much more alive you will feel and it will become clear to you that you were only existing before and experiencing very little of those around you. If you have children, remember back to the first moments of silent communication. Those unspoken moments with a little one who could not yet speak were so powerful and so full of love imparted by nothing but a loving look into a new soul. This is a communication that we reserve only for those we are sure are in love with us already because it isn't safe to "speak" this way to others—or is it? Bombshells know the power of this kind of interaction in every day life and we understand what it can accomplish for all those who choose to embrace the energy being shared with them.

CHAPTER SIXTEEN

Bombshell Forever

CHAPTER SIXTEEN
Bombshell Forever

I was close to finishing this book when I was on a plane back from Florida—a late flight, not due to arrive until after midnight, so I was anxious to settle in. Upon getting to my seat I was greeted by the lady sitting next to me, a beautiful, vibrant, funny woman enjoying a glass of champagne. She was certainly my kind of woman! What I didn't realize was that I was in the presence of an eighty-six-year-old Bombshell. It's not that I didn't think it was possible; it's just that I had never met one before. I was in for a three-hour treat and wisdom that I will always be grateful for.

I felt so happy being in her company and she in mine. I realized that this was what all women could look forward to if they chose. Hazel dances almost weekly, she says that when she hears a "number with a good beat" she can scarcely help it. She laughs easily and melodiously in a way that made me sure she has chosen to laugh all the way through her eighty-six years. Her spirit is so strong that it transports those in her presence and they forget that she was born in 1918. Clearly she knows that hers is a gift to be given generously and without condition. You can feel it!

Hazel was wearing some pretty cool jeans and a white sweatshirt that you may see on someone far less than half her age, but she was able to pull it off without losing the grace of her years. "I like to keep up with the times, you know," she continues, "I don't know why people get stuck in a rut. All kinds of fashions can be modified to suit a lady." She talks the talk and walks the walk and was insulted that the airline insisted she board the plane in a wheelchair. If only they could see her at the local dance hall where she hangs out with the thirty-year-old friends she likes to keep! Make no mistake, Hazel knows things that most people only hope to understand and she doesn't miss a beat on the dance floor or in a conversation either.

Being one of those women who refused to sit at home and wilt while her male counterpart was out there in the working world, Hazel decided she was going to shine in the business world, as well as in her home and social life. She loves people and her love of meeting new and interesting individuals prompted her to open her own dry cleaning business.

She tells me that she "loved every day meeting all those folks" and I would hazard a guess that those who were lucky enough to have dealings with her loved her as well. Eventually, Hazel had a number of locations—a feat unheard of in her day. "I always had a head for business. It was in my blood," she tells me with well-deserved pride.

I meet Hazel and her equally beautiful and sparkly sister, Francis, for lunch. It is the history and perspectives of these women that deepen my belief that Bombshells are ageless and that their grace only becomes more alluring with every passing year. Francis is older than Hazel, yet it seems to me that Hazel was the one who had taken on the roles of leadership and fearlessness. Even though the years they spent growing up in a small mining town made them very close, there was a clear and distinct dynamic playing out between them. "I was what they called 'delicate,'" Hazel tells me, Francis nodding in agreement. "I remember our mother having company over and seeing Francis standing at the front door, her beautiful, thick, curly hair and healthy pink cheeks," Hazel describes her sister admiringly. People always commented on how beautiful Hazel's sisters were and she knew that their appearance was drastically different from her own, more fragile features. "Even when I knew they were the pretty ones I raced to the front door to take my place, proudly thrusting my face forward, hoping they would say something good!" They generally reserved the same, polite remarks for Hazel's pale face and white hair, perhaps not even knowing that she was aware of the distinction between her and her sisters. She knew she was not receiving the same accolades that her sisters elicited. It is funny though, Hazel was a Bombshell in the making even then and she was only inspired to expand her shine and show the world her unstoppable spirit. Just hearing the stories and being an audience to these two eighty-something women was a lesson in life and soul for me. Despite being considered the more beautiful of the two, Francis was in open admiration of her sister and would often speak quietly through Hazel, as though the delivery of her words through Hazel would somehow be more meaningful.

These women were raised by extremely loving and progressive parents. When I asked Hazel about her family she seemed to go off to a place where she could actually see the images of her parents and recall the days of her childhood with nothing but the greatest pleasure. "Oh, my mother!" she exclaimed breathlessly. "She made everything a party." Hazel conveys the gifts of joy and freedom of the soul instilled by her mother. "She taught us how to laugh and spread joy, not just to each other, but to all," she says. Clearly this relationship was a part of a wonderful foundation on which this confident, radiant, sparkling Bombshell could grow, illustrating this as a gift to be uncovered as soon as possible so it can be enjoyed and shared as much as possible in one lifetime.

AFTERWORD
It's a Bombshell's World

I am sure this has, and will continue to be, an interesting journey filled with personal evolution and the realization that you really are the Bombshell we all can be. The life of a Bombshell is about making choices for yourself and those around you that allow for the best balance between being the best woman and person you can be. It is not about judging others; the only yardstick you need to measure yourself by is that which you have created for your own life. The guidance and support of others may certainly play a role in your transformation, but ultimately dear Bombshell, it will be the contents of your heart and soul that will inspire you to shine.

The looks and mannerisms of others will be things that can inspire you to uncover those qualities within yourself, but they are not to be imitated, only emulated after discovering your own. This is not a book about personal perfection because every good Bombshell knows that this does not exist (but for the hand of a very skilled airbrush artist); this is a book about being perfectly happy with who you are as a woman. You will come to discover the ways in which you have been stifling your beauty and sparkle and then you will vow never to do it again! Your days of shrinking into a crowd will be a thing of the past and will only be revisited in order to inspire someone else to their own magnificence.

Take care of yourself as the woman you are evolving into and give yourself permission to embrace the things that you have historically tried to hide. The strength you gain from allowing yourself these imperfections will be both liberating and enlightening to your journey. The only time that these things can be a detriment is when you fear them or run from them—the Bombshell does neither of these. We are long past the time when we attempted to fade out and hide behind the disillusions of our comfort zone and recognize that the comfort zone is for women who are a little afraid of themselves and life in general. We Bombshells understand that reaching beyond our comfort zone is a little like the child reaching for the off-limits cookie jar—we are just far enough away that when we experience the sweetness we were craving its flavor is heightened exponentially. If those cookies were out in plain view on the counter they would lose their allure.

Life is like this; the things that are the most difficult to acquire will be the most valuable to you in life. If there were a pill to take for the transformation, every woman would already be a Bombshell because everyone wants to feel special and sparkly, so taking the steps to make that happen for yourself should be second nature once you make the decision to look into yourself for those Bombshell qualities. Happiness and self love will become your new comfort zone.

Maybe some women are afraid that they won't find what they are looking for, maybe this is why some of them allow the flannel blanket of mediocrity to wrap itself around them, but this does not make the best of their potential. I, as the Bombshell Coach, with this book, am here to tell you that all women have the potential shine and sparkle of a Bombshell. This isn't a hit and miss proposition. You all have what it takes to glow and excel in ways that will make you, happier, healthier people. It was the gift given to all of us when we opened our eyes to the world as women; some of us choose to nurture it right away, and some don't. What matters now is that you are making the choice to excavate yourself from the cement of society's misgivings and see what your true potential is. Some women were born into families and cultures that attempted to stifle the rising tide of glorious femininity, but I promise you Bombshell, that you will have your chance to shine. Don't let negative people or experiences rob you of sharing your gifts with the world. You can find the things that you most value about yourself and combine those with the acceptance of the things you once feared, and when melded together you can form an emotional compound that will last you a lifetime, an unshakeable and beautiful mixture so unique that others in your life will want to know your recipe, your secret.

It will become incumbent upon you to share some of your secrets with other women, just as I have in this book. Although I have admittedly kept a few things for myself, I want every woman in the world to take a look at herself and begin her own Bombshell transformation, not trying to be the most beautiful or the thinnest or even the most intelligent woman in the world, but the most intelligent, prettiest and most healthy woman possible for you.

This is a journey about perfecting you and only measuring yourself by how you once felt as opposed to how you will feel at the end of the transition. It is quite like the woman who loses 150 pounds and still weighs 175; it doesn't matter that for some women this would be miserable because for her it is an amazing accomplishment and she will emanate her feelings of self satisfaction. Her shine will come not by being a size two, but in not being an unhealthy size twenty-two. The times in her life when this woman was a twenty-two, she was unable to approach people socially or for career advancement are no longer because she has a renewed sense of self-confidence that will continue to be the key to her winning smile and her celebration of her soul. It is the cumulative effects of these wonderful changes that combine to alter everything in life when you make the choice and allow the transformation to begin and continue to work towards progress.

Let them look. Let them whisper. Let them wonder. Revel in this attention and embrace it as part of the new world you have discovered. Any time you feel overwhelmed or intimidated by all of the attention you receive, think back to your days of anonymity. Think back to when you felt as though your presence wouldn't be missed if you evaporated. Now look at the woman you have discovered—beautiful and sexy in your own skin, embracing every flaw and celebrating every success. You are new; new to the parts of yourself you forgot were there, new in your confidence and open attitude toward those you choose to allow into your world.

I have had so many people ask why I teach the things that I do and why I give away the secrets of my happiness. The simple answer is that I do it because I want every woman in the world to know that she can see the changes happen within herself if she is willing to try. I have seen the potential to sparkle in every woman I have every met—every woman. This is not about size, shape, blondes or brunettes. It is about women. All women. I want them to shine because of the way I know it will enrich themselves, their lives and the lives of those around them. It will show them how to shine just as I was shown how to do so by my own mother. I was lucky because I was born into a home where I was taught how to shine and I was given permission, and indeed encouraged, to sparkle. Most women aren't this lucky, perhaps they were raised to subscribe to the insecurities of our society, or maybe a relationship stifled the natural flow of their own wondrous gifts but whatever the impediment it is now cast aside—permanently.

Whatever the case Bombshell, make no apologies for your newfound strength. Never let go of the milestones you've already reached and don't stop looking for new ones. It is all about finding the things in yourself that you didn't know existed, the shine and the sparkle you've had since you were born a glorious woman. Let womanhood bring you motherhood if you choose but don't allow one to cancel out the other. Be the most wonderful friend and life partner you can without sacrificing the celebration of your soul. Don't regret those you are forced to leave behind and know that they may catch up someday. Do share yourself, your gifts and your flaws, as they are all part of a magical combination that is uniquely you. Be a size two, twelve or twenty-two but still know that the size of your body will only shrink when beside the size of your heart. Be a Bombshell—blonde, brunette, fiery red, that doesn't matter as much as the color of your soul.

Jacqueline Bradley- The Bombshell Coach- has appeared across North America on shows such as,

- Style By Jury
- Yummy Mummy
- CTV Your Health
- City TV
- CFRB 1010

She is available for speaking engagements

For information on The Bombshell Coach please go to

www.thebombshellbible.com

*For a 10% discount on packages or Bombshell Merchandise please quote the isbn number of this book.

Jacqueline

The Bombshell Coach

www.thebombshellbible.com